はしがき

　本書は第一学習社発行の英語教科書「CREATIVE English Communication Ⅱ」に完全準拠したノートです。各パート見開き 2 ページで，主に教科書本文の予習や授業傍用での使用に役立つよう工夫しました。

CONTENTS

本書の構成と利用法

本書は教科書本文を完全に理解するための学習の導きをしています。本書を最大限に活用して，教科書本文の理解を深めましょう。

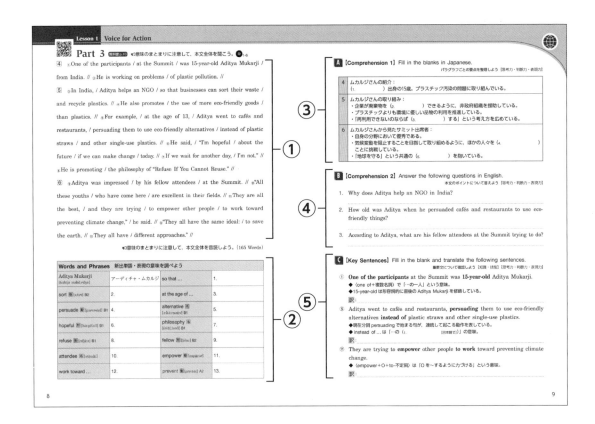

① 教科書本文

意味のまとまりごとにスラッシュ (/) を入れました。ここで示した意味のまとまりを意識しながら音読しましょう。また学習がしやすいよう，一文ずつ番号を付けました。上部の二次元コードは本文音声のリスニングや音読に使用できる「スピーキング・トレーナー」にリンクしています。右ページに詳しい解説があります。

　※本文中の　グレーのマーカー　は，教科書では印字されておらず，音声としてのみ配信している部分であることを示します。

　※◉₀₀は，生徒用音声CD（別売）のディスク番号とトラック番号を示します。

② Words and Phrases

新出単語・表現の意味を調べて，意味を日本語で記入しましょう。単語の品詞と発音記号も示しました。A1〜B2は，CEFR-Jでのレベルを示します。色の付いた単語は，読んで意味がわかるだけでなく，表現活動でも使えるようにしておきたい語です。

『CEFR-J Wordlist Version 1.6』東京外国語大学投野由紀夫研究室.
（URL: http://cefr-j.org/download.html より2021年2月ダウンロード）

③ **A** 問

　図表を日本語で完成させることで本文の理解を深める問題です。地図・グラフなど，パートごとにさまざまな形の図表を完成させます。

④ **B** 問

　教科書本文に関連する英語の質問に対し，英語で答える問題です。教科書の **Q** とは別の問題としています。**A** 問で完成させた図表がヒントになる問題も含まれています。

⑤ **C** 問

　教科書の各文で，新出の文法事項や「Focus on Five Skill Areas」に関連したもの，また文構造が複雑なものや指示語を含むものなどを重要文と位置づけ，解説を加えました。解説を日本語や英語で完成させ，和訳をする問題です。

Web コンテンツ

スピーキング・トレーナー

本文の音声データ無料配信，音読用のボイスレコーダーが使用できます。

https://dg-w.jp/b/74a0012

音声データ配信

・音声データを無料でダウンロード，または再生ができます。音声ファイルは MP3形式，一括ダウンロードは ZIP 形式になっております。

　＊アップしてある音声データは著作権法で保護されています。音声データの利用は個人が私的に利用する場合に限られます。データを第三者に提供・販売することはできません。

ボイスレコーダー　アクセスキー：wt3yp

・音読の学習効果をさらに高めるために，自分の発話の録音ができるボイスレコーダーを用意しました。PC やスマートフォンからご利用できます。

　ボイスレコーダーの使用にはユーザー ID とパスワードが必要です。ID とパスワードを自分で設定（半角英数字5文字以上）して，利用を開始してください。

メモ欄

ID	
パスワード	

＊ ID とパスワードは紛失しないようにしてください。万が一紛失した場合は，それまでに記録された学習履歴がすべて参照できなくなります。復元はできませんので，ご注意ください。

＊正常に動作しない場合は「ヘルプ」→「動作要件」をご確認ください。

Part 1

教科書 p.6〜p.7 🔊意味のまとまりに注意して，本文全体を聞こう。 ◉1-2

①You are learning / about climate change. // ②On the Internet, / you find an article / about a high school student / who is working / on environmentally sustainable development. //

③Eva Jones, / an American female student / from Hood River Valley High School, / attended the United Nations Youth Climate Summit. // ④She was one of the 500 young people / selected to join the Summit. // ⑤She was also one of the 100 "Green Ticket" winners; / the United Nations Fund / supported her trip / to this event. //

⑥I grew up / in the Columbia Gorge / in the U.S. // ⑦There are different communities / and environments there. // ⑧I was inspired to be an advocate / for the earth / and the living things / on it. //

⑨I'm honored / to be selected / as a voice at the Summit. // ⑩Brave action / is the only way / to make a difference / for future generations. // ⑪We must have our leaders / take responsibility / seriously. //

⑫We have the power / to stop the bad effects / that are changing the earth's climate. // ⑬The main way is / to use our money / for encouraging sustainable consumption / and for stopping the use / of unclean energy. // ⑭I'm proud / to represent my lovely hometown / and the environmental beauty / I grew up in. //

🔊意味のまとまりに注意して，本文全体を音読しよう。（192 Words）

Words and Phrases	新出単語・表現の意味を調べよう		
environmentally 副 [ɪnvàɪ(ə)r(ə)nmént(ə)li] B2	1.	sustainable 形 [səstéɪnəb(ə)l]	2.
development 名 [dɪvéləpmənt] B1	3.	Eva Jones [íːvə dʒóʊnz]	エヴァ・ジョーンズ
female 形[fíːmeɪl] A2	4.	Hood River Valley [húd rívər vǽli]	フッドリバーバレー
attend 動[əténd] B1	5.	youth 名[júːθ] A2	6.
summit 名[sʌ́mɪt] B1	7.	select ... to 〜	8.
Columbia Gorge [kəlʌ́mbiə góːrdʒ]	コロンビア峡谷	be inspired to 〜	9.

honor 動 [á(:)nər] B2	10.	be honored to ～	11.
make a difference	12.	take responsibility	13.
effect 名 [ɪfékt] A2	14.	consumption 名 [kənsʌ́m(p)ʃ(ə)n] B1	15.
unclean 形 [ʌ̀nklíːn]	16.	represent 動 [rèprɪzént] A2	17.

A 【Comprehension 1】 Fill in the blanks in Japanese.　要点を整理しよう【思考力・判断力・表現力】

記事で紹介されている高校生	エヴァ・ジョーンズさんの思い
◆名前：エヴァ・ジョーンズ	・故郷であるアメリカ合衆国のコロンビア峡谷にはさまざまな地域社会や環境があり，自分は地球やその生物の（4.　　　　　）になりたい。
◆性別：（1.　　　　　）	・（5.　　　　　）行動が将来の世代のために変化を起こす唯一の方法。指導者たちに本気で責任をとってもらわなければならない。
◆出身高校：フッドリバーバレー高校	・私たちは地球の気候を変化させている悪影響を止める（6.　　　　）を持っている。
◆どのような人か： ・国連ユース気候サミットの参加者として選ばれた（2.　　　　）人のうちの一人 ・「グリーンチケット」を獲得した（3.　　　　）人のうちの一人	

B 【Comprehension 2】 Answer the following questions in English.
本文のポイントについて答えよう【思考力・判断力・表現力】

1. Where did Eva grow up?

---

2. How does Eva feel about representing her hometown and its environmental beauty?

C 【Key Sentences】 Translate the following sentences.
重要文について確認しよう【知識・技能】【思考力・判断力・表現力】

⑪ We must **have** our leaders **take** responsibility seriously.
　◆使役動詞 have は〈have＋O＋原形不定詞〉で「O に～してもらう」という意味。
　訳：

⑬ The main way is **to use** our money for encouraging sustainable consumption and for stopping the use of unclean energy.
　◆to use は to-不定詞の名詞用法で，「使うこと」という意味。
　◆接続詞 and は前後にある2つの前置詞句 for ... をつないでいる。
　訳：

5

Part 2 教科書p.8 ◁意味のまとまりに注意して，本文全体を聞こう。 ◎1-4

①Climate change / is one of the biggest environmental problems. // ②These days, / the need to deal with it / is becoming increasingly urgent. //

① ③The United Nations Youth Climate Summit / took place / on September 21, / 2019. // ④It was held / at the UN Headquarters / located in New York. // ⑤Young climate action leaders / presented their ideas / to politicians / all over the world. // ⑥The Youth Climate Summit / was followed / by the UN Climate Action Summit / on September 23. //

② ⑦Over 7,000 young people / from more than 140 countries and territories / applied to the Youth Climate Summit. // ⑧They were selected / on the basis of how they worked / on climate change / and discussed possible solutions. // ⑨Their performances were evaluated / by a panel / led by UN officials. // ⑩After that, / 500 of the young people / were invited to the Summit. // ⑪One hundred of them / got "Green Tickets." // ⑫These winners received / fully funded travel / to New York. // ⑬Their transportation / was as carbon-neutral / as possible. // ⑭In other words, / they used vehicles / which emitted less carbon dioxide. //

③ ⑮The participants shared their ideas / on the global stage. // ⑯They delivered / a clear message / to world leaders: / We need to act now / to work / on climate change. //

◁意味のまとまりに注意して，本文全体を音読しよう。（190 Words）

Words and Phrases	新出単語・表現の意味を調べよう		
these days	1.	deal 動[díːl] B1	2.
deal with …	3.	increasingly 副 [ɪnkríːsɪŋli] B1	4.
urgent 形[ə́ːrdʒ(ə)nt] B1	5.	take place	6.
headquarters 名 [hédkwɔ̀ːrtərz] B2	7.	locate 動[lóʊkeɪt] B1	8.
territory 名[térətɔ̀ːri] B2	9.	apply 動[əplái] A2	10.
apply to …	11.	on the basis of …	12.

evaluate 動[ɪvǽljuèɪt] B2	13.	panel 名[pǽn(ə)l] B2	14.
as … as possible	15.	carbon-neutral 形 [kὰ:rb(ə)nnjú:tr(ə)l]	16.
in other words	17.	vehicle 名[ví:ək(ə)l] B1	18.
emit 動[ɪmít]	19.	participant 名 [pərtísɪp(ə)nt] B1	20.

A 【Comprehension 1】 Fill in the blanks in Japanese.

パラグラフごとの要点を整理しよう【思考力・判断力・表現力】

1	国連ユース気候サミット： ・いつ：2019年（1.　　　）月21日　　　・どこで：国連本部（ニューヨーク） ・だれが：若手の気候問題に取り組む活動家 ・何をしたか：世界の（2.　　　　　　）に対して自分の考えを発表した
2	サミットの選考過程： ◆（3.　　　）以上の国や地域から7,000人を超える若い人たちが応募した。　➡　◆そのうち（4.　　　）人がサミットに招待された。　➡　◆そのうち100人が「グリーンチケット」を獲得し，ニューヨークへの全額の旅費を受け取った。 ◆移動手段はできる限りの（5.　　　　　　）なものだった。
3	サミット出席者がしたこと： ・世界の舞台で自分たちの考えを共有した。 ・「私たちは（6.　　　　　　）に取り組むために，今行動する必要がある」というメッセージを世界の指導者たちに伝えた。

B 【Comprehension 2】 Answer the following questions in English.

本文のポイントについて答えよう【思考力・判断力・表現力】

1. Where was the United Nations Youth Climate Summit held?

   ----

2. What did "Green Ticket" winners receive?

C 【Key Sentences】 Translate the following sentence.

重要文について確認しよう【知識・技能】【思考力・判断力・表現力】

⑧ They were selected on the basis of **how they worked on climate change** and discussed possible solutions.

　　◆〈疑問詞＋S＋V〉から成る疑問詞節が，文中で名詞節の働きをしている。
　　◆and は worked と discussed の 2 つの動詞句を結んでいる。
　　訳：--

Part 3 教科書 p.10 ◁意味のまとまりに注意して，本文全体を聞こう。 ◎1-6

④ ①One of the participants / at the Summit / was 15-year-old Aditya Mukarji / from India. // ②He is working on problems / of plastic pollution. //

⑤ ③In India, / Aditya helps an NGO / so that businesses can sort their waste / and recycle plastics. // ④He also promotes / the use of more eco-friendly goods / than plastics. // ⑤For example, / at the age of 13, / Aditya went to cafés and restaurants, / persuading them to use eco-friendly alternatives / instead of plastic straws / and other single-use plastics. // ⑥He said, / "I'm hopeful / about the future / if we can make change / today. // ⑦If we wait for another day, / I'm not." // ⑧He is promoting / the philosophy of "Refuse If You Cannot Reuse." //

⑥ ⑨Aditya was impressed / by his fellow attendees / at the Summit. // ⑩"All these youths / who have come here / are excellent in their fields. // ⑪They are all the best, / and they are trying / to empower other people / to work toward preventing climate change," / he said. // ⑫"They all have the same ideal: / to save the earth. // ⑬They all have / different approaches." //

◁意味のまとまりに注意して，本文全体を音読しよう。（165 Words）

Words and Phrases	新出単語・表現の意味を調べよう		
Aditya Mukarji [áːdɪtjə məkɑ́ːrdʒə]	アーディチャ・ムカルジ	so that …	1.
sort 動 [sɔ́ːrt] B2	2.	at the age of …	3.
persuade 動 [pərswéɪd] B1	4.	alternative 名 [ɔːltə́ːrnətɪv] B1	5.
hopeful 形 [hóʊpf(ə)l] B1	6.	philosophy 名 [fəlá(ː)səfi] B1	7.
refuse 動 [rɪfjúːz] B1	8.	fellow 形 [félou] B2	9.
attendee 名 [ətèndíː]	10.	empower 動 [ɪmpáʊər]	11.
work toward …	12.	prevent 動 [prɪvént] A2	13.

A 【Comprehension 1】 Fill in the blanks in Japanese.

パラグラフごとの要点を整理しよう【思考力・判断力・表現力】

4	ムカルジさんの紹介： (1.) 出身の15歳。プラスチック汚染の問題に取り組んでいる。
5	ムカルジさんの取り組み： ・企業が廃棄物を（2. ）できるように，非政府組織を援助している。 ・プラスチックよりも環境に優しい品物の利用を推進している。 ・「再利用できないのならば（3. ）する」という考え方を広めている。
6	ムカルジさんから見たサミット出席者： ・自身の分野において優秀である。 ・気候変動を阻止することを目指して取り組めるように，ほかの人々を（4. ） ことに挑戦している。 ・「地球を守る」という共通の（5. ）を抱いている。

B 【Comprehension 2】 Answer the following questions in English.

本文のポイントについて答えよう【思考力・判断力・表現力】

1. Why does Aditya help an NGO in India?

   ----

2. How old was Aditya when he persuaded cafés and restaurants to use eco-friendly things?

   ----

3. According to Aditya, what are his fellow attendees at the Summit trying to do?

C 【Key Sentences】 Fill in the blank and translate the following sentences.

重要文について確認しよう【知識・技能】【思考力・判断力・表現力】

① **One of the participants** at the Summit was **15-year-old** Aditya Mukarji.
   ◆〈one of＋複数名詞〉で「…の一人」という意味。
   ◆15-year-old は形容詞的に直後の Aditya Mukarji を修飾している。
   訳:---

⑤ Aditya went to cafés and restaurants, **persuading** them to use eco-friendly alternatives **instead of** plastic straws and other single-use plastics.
   ◆現在分詞 persuading で始まる句が，連続して起こる動作を表している。
   ◆ instead of ... は「…の（1.   [日本語で]）」の意味。
   訳:---

⑪ They are trying to **empower** other people **to work** toward preventing climate change.
   ◆〈empower＋O＋to-不定詞〉は「O を～するように力づける」という意味。
   訳:---

Part 4 教科書p.11 ◁意味のまとまりに注意して，本文全体を聞こう。 ◉1-8

[7] ①Fifteen-year-old Lesein Mathenge Mutunkei / from Kenya / also joined the Summit. // ②He belonged to a soccer team / and began his "Trees4Goals" activity / in 2018. // ③"I used to plant one tree / for every goal / I scored. // ④But now / I plant 11 trees / for every goal," / said Lesein. // ⑤He has planted / more than 1,400 trees. // ⑥He also keeps track of the places / where he planted the trees / so that he can make sure / that they are growing. //

[8] ⑦Lesein respects Wangari Maathai, / a Kenyan environmental activist. // ⑧She took the initiative / in planting trees / in Africa. // ⑨He always keeps her words / in mind: / "I will be / a hummingbird; / I will do / the best I can." // ⑩In an Ecuadorean folk tale, / only the little hummingbird / tried to protect the forest / from a big fire. //

[9] ⑪Lesein wants to learn / new ways / to help save the planet. // ⑫"Maathai did her part, / and now / it is time / for young people / to do their part. // ⑬Any little thing we do / can be a help. // ⑭Planting a tree, / picking up litter, / or even sharing information / on the Internet / ... everything counts," / he says. //

◁意味のまとまりに注意して，本文全体を音読しよう。(182 Words)

Words and Phrases 新出単語・表現の意味を調べよう			
Lesein Mathenge Mutunkei [ləséɪn məθéŋɡə mətənkéɪ]	ルセイン・マセンゲ・ムトゥンケイ	Kenya 名 [kénjə]	1.
belong 動 [bɪlɔ́ːŋ] A2	2.	belong to ...	3.
keep track of ...	4.	Wangari Maathai [wəŋɡáːri mɑːtái]	ワンガリ・マータイ
Kenyan 形 [kénjən]	5.	activist 名 [ǽktɪvɪst]	6.
initiative 名 [ɪníʃətɪv] B2	7.	take the initiative in ...	8.
keep ... in mind	9.	hummingbird 名 [hʌ́mɪŋbə̀ːrd]	10.
Ecuadorean 形 [èkwədɔ́ːriən]	11.	tale 名 [téɪl] B1	12.
protect A from B	13.	do one's part	14.
litter 名 [lítər] B2	15.		

A 【Comprehension 1】 Fill in the blanks in Japanese.

パラグラフごとの要点を整理しよう【思考力・判断力・表現力】

7	ムトゥンケイさんの「Trees4Goals」活動： ・(1. 　　　　　) 年に開始した。 ・サッカーで得点したゴール1つにつき (2. 　　　　　) 本の木を植えている。 ・木を植えた場所の記録を続けている。
8	ワンガリ・マータイについて： ・ワンガリ・マータイ：ケニアの環境 (3. 　　　　　) 家 ・マータイの言葉：「私はハチドリになろうと思う。私はできる限り最善を尽くそうと思う。」 ・エクアドルの民話：小さなハチドリだけが森を大規模な (4. 　　　　) から守ろうとした。
9	ムトゥンケイさんのメッセージ： ・今，若い人たちが自身の役目を果たすときである。 ・私たちがするどんな小さなことでも助けになりえる。木を植えることや (5. 　　　　　) を拾うこと，インターネットで情報を (6. 　　　　　) することなど。

B 【Comprehension 2】 Answer the following questions in English.

本文のポイントについて答えよう【思考力・判断力・表現力】

1. How many trees does Lesein plant for every goal he scores?

　　...

2. Where did Wangari Maathai step forward in planting trees?

　　...

3. In an Ecuadorean folk tale, what did the hummingbird try to do?

　　...

C 【Key Sentences】 Fill in the blank and translate the following sentences.

重要文について確認しよう【知識・技能】【思考力・判断力・表現力】

③ I **used to** plant one tree for every goal (I scored).

　◆ used to ～は過去の習慣を表して (1. 　　　　　　　　　　[日本語で]) という意味。

　◆ S＋V で構成される I scored は every goal を修飾する。関係代名詞が省略されていると考えてもよい。

　訳：...

⑥ He also **keeps track of** the places (**where** he planted the trees) **so that** he can make sure that they are growing.

　◆関係副詞 where を含む節が，先行詞 the places を修飾する。

　◆ keep track of ... は「…の記録をする [続ける]」の意味。so that ... は「…するように」という「目的」の意味。

　訳：...

11

Lesson 1　Voice for Action

Activity Plus　教科書 p.16～p.17　◁意味のまとまりに注意して，本文全体を聞こう。◎ 1-10

①In an English class, / a teacher and three students are speaking / at a mock youth climate summit. // ②You are listening / to them. //

Teacher: ③Here / we have three excellent climate activists. // ④Now, / please share your actions / for protecting the environment. // ⑤Will you start, / Kazuki? //

Kazuki: ⑥Well, / I'm interested / in engineering. // ⑦I read a book / about an African boy / who made a windmill / that generates electricity. // ⑧We need / renewable energy sources / to replace generators / which use fossil fuels. //

Teacher: ⑨So, / Kazuki, / you believe / that we must replace fossil fuels / with more eco-friendly energy sources. // ⑩Next, / can you tell us / what you're doing, / Emily? //

Emily: ⑪I'm planning / to write a letter / to convince our school's administration / to install solar panels. // ⑫I started looking for supporters / and have found teachers and friends / who agree with my idea. // ⑬The more supporters I have, / the stronger my appeal will become. //

Teacher: ⑭Thank you, / Emily! // ⑮You're saying / that finding more supporters for your idea / is the key. // ⑯Satoshi, / how about you? // ⑰What action / are you taking? //

Satoshi: ⑱I started studying economics / as well as environmental issues. // ⑲Some world leaders are saying / that young activists should calm down / and study economics first. // ⑳If I have some knowledge / about economics, / my ideas about environmental issues / will be more convincing. //

Teacher: ㉑I see, / Satoshi. // ㉒Your point is / that it is important / to make your opinion persuasive. //

◁意味のまとまりに注意して，本文全体を音読しよう。(219 Words)

Words and Phrases	新出単語・表現の意味を調べよう		
mock 形 [má(:)k] B2	1.	windmill 名 [wín(d)mìl]	2.
generate 動 [dʒénərèɪt] B1	3.	renewable 形 [rɪnjúːəb(ə)l]	4.
generator 名 [dʒénərèɪtər]	5.	replace A with B	6.
convince 動 [kənvíns] B1	7.	administration 名 [ədmìnɪstréɪʃ(ə)n] B1	8.
supporter 名 [səpɔ́ːrtər] B1	9.	appeal 名 [əpíːl] B1	10.

12

take action	11.	economics 名 [ì:kəná(:)mɪks] B1	12.
A as well as B	13.	issue 名[íʃuː] A2	14.
calm down	15.	knowledge 名 [ná(:)lɪdʒ] A2	16.
persuasive 形 [pərswéɪsɪv] B1	17.		

A 【Comprehension 1】 Fill in the blanks in Japanese. 要点を整理しよう【思考力・判断力・表現力】

発表者	行動［事実］	考え［意見］
カズキ	発電する（1.　　　　　　）を作ったアフリカの少年に関する本を読んだ。	私たちには化石燃料を使う発電機に代わる，（2.　　　　　　）なエネルギー源が必要だ。
エミリー	学校の理事会に（3.　　　　　　）を設置することに納得してもらうための手紙を書くことを計画している。	多くの（4.　　　　　　）がいればいるほど，自分の訴えは説得力のあるものになっていく。
サトシ	環境問題とあわせて（5.　　　　　　）を学び始めた。	もし（5.　　　　　）の知識が増えれば，環境問題についての自分の考えはもっと（6.　　　　　　）が増す。

B 【Comprehension 2】 Answer the following questions in English.

本文のポイントについて答えよう【思考力・判断力・表現力】

1. In Kazuki's opinion, what do we need to replace generators which use fossil fuels?

....

2. Why is Emily planning to write a letter to her school's administration?

....

C 【Key Sentences】 Translate the following sentences.

重要文について確認しよう【知識・技能】【思考力・判断力・表現力】

⑦ I read a book about an African boy (who made a windmill (that generates electricity)).

◆関係代名詞 who を含む節が，先行詞 an African boy を修飾する。

◆ who で始まる関係詞節内でも同様に，関係代名詞 that を含む節が，先行詞 a windmill を修飾する。

訳:...

⑬ **The more supporters** I have, **the stronger** my appeal will become.

◆ 〈the＋比較級＋S＋V …, the＋比較級＋S＋V 〜〉は「…すればするほど〜」という比例の関係。

訳:...

Part 1　教科書 p.22～p.23　◀意味のまとまりに注意して，本文全体を聞こう。◎1-12

① You and your friend / are visiting a zoo. // ② At the entrance, / you are given / a picture card / which shows the lifestyles / of three animals. // ③ On the card, / each animal asks you / to guess what animal / it is. //

④ Who Am I? //

⑤ The answer to each "Who Am I?" question is / in front of our cages. //

⑥ Please come and see us! //

　⑦ Animal No.1 //

⑧ I almost always live / in a tree / and seldom descend / to the ground. // ⑨ I only eat / the leaves of a specific tree, / and I usually don't drink / water. // ⑩ I don't like moving around, / but I like sleeping / very much. // ⑪ I sleep / about 20 hours / a day. // ⑫ Who am I? //

　⑬ Animal No.2 //

⑭ I am very tall, / and I like eating the leaves / of tall trees. // ⑮ I have to eat / a large amount of leaves / every day. // ⑯ My tongue can extend / up to 50 centimeters / out of my mouth, / so I can take many leaves / off a branch / at a time. // ⑰ I only sleep / about two hours / a day / because I am busy eating. // ⑱ Who am I? //

　⑲ Animal No.3 //

⑳ The rainforest is my home / and I never go down / to the ground. // ㉑ I don't have a family, / and I live / all by myself. // ㉒ I have long arms / that are about twice as long / as my legs. // ㉓ My favorite food / is fruit. // ㉔ I make a bed / to sleep in / with branches I take / from trees. // ㉕ Who am I? //

◀意味のまとまりに注意して，本文全体を音読しよう。（236 Words）

Words and Phrases　新出単語・表現の意味を調べよう			
lifestyle 名 [láɪfstàɪl] A2	1.	orangutan 名 [ɔːrǽŋətæ̀n]	2.
giraffe 名 [dʒərǽf] B1	3.	capybara 名 [kæ̀pəbɑ́(ː)rə]	4.
seldom 副 [séldəm] B2	5.	descend 動 [dɪsénd] B2	6.
tongue 名 [tʌ́ŋ] B1	7.	extend 動 [ɪksténd] B1	8.
up to …	9.	take A off B	10.

branch 图[bræn(t)ʃ] A2	11.	at a time	12.
be busy ～ing	13.	rainforest 图 [réɪnfɔ̀ːrəst] B1	14.
take A from B	15.		

A 【Comprehension 1】 Fill in the blanks in Japanese.

要点を整理しよう【思考力・判断力・表現力】

3種の動物の（1.　　　　　　）の違い

動物	生活する場所	食べ物	睡眠時間
No.1	ほとんどいつも木の上	（2.　　　）の木の葉のみ	約20時間
No.2		木の葉	およそ（3.　　　）時間
No.3	（4.　　　　　　　　　） の木の上	（5.　　　　　）が大好物	

B 【Comprehension 2】 Answer the following questions in English.

本文のポイントについて答えよう【思考力・判断力・表現力】

1. How many hours does Animal No.1 sleep a day?

　---

2. Why does Animal No.2 sleep so little?

　---

3. How long are the arms of Animal No.3?

C 【Key Sentences】 Translate the following sentences.

重要文について確認しよう【知識・技能】【思考力・判断力・表現力】

② At the entrance, you are given a picture card (which shows the lifestyles of three animals).

　◆関係代名詞 which を含む節が，先行詞 a picture card を修飾する。

　訳：---

㉒ I have long arms (that are about **twice as long as** my legs).

　◆that は long arms を先行詞とする関係代名詞。
　◆〈twice as＋形容詞［副詞］原級＋as ...〉で，「…の２倍の～」という意味。

　訳：---

Part 2 教科書 p.24 🔊意味のまとまりに注意して，本文全体を聞こう。 ◎1-14

①How long do animals sleep? // ②Do most animals sleep / as long as human beings do / every day? //

1 ③In general, / human beings need / seven to eight hours of sleep / every night / in order to stay healthy. // ④This means / that we spend / about one third of our whole life / sleeping. // ⑤However, / what about other animals? // ⑥Sleeping time varies / greatly / from animal to animal. // ⑦For instance, / koalas sleep / for about 20 hours / a day, / but giraffes' sleeping time / is amazingly short / —— only about two hours / a day. //

2 ⑧Koalas mostly live / in trees, / and they feed, / sleep or rest / most of the time. // ⑨They eat / only eucalyptus leaves. // ⑩The leaves have / a high water content / but are poor / in nutrition. // ⑪Therefore, / koalas don't get / enough energy / from their diet / to move around much. //

3 ⑫Eucalyptus leaves / also contain toxins / that are hard / for other animals / to remove. // ⑬Koalas can get rid of / these toxins, / but it takes a lot of energy / to do that. // ⑭It is thought / that they save energy / by doing nothing / besides eating / and resting. //

🔊意味のまとまりに注意して，本文全体を音読しよう。（174 Words）

Words and Phrases 新出単語・表現の意味を調べよう			
general 形[dʒén(ə)r(ə)l] B1	1.	in general	2.
vary 動[véəri] B1	3.	instance 名[ínst(ə)ns] B1	4.
for instance	5.	mostly 副[móus(t)li] A2	6.
eucalyptus 名[jùːkəlíptəs]	7.	content 名[ká(ː)ntent] B1	8.
nutrition 名[njuːtríʃ(ə)n] B1	9.	therefore 副[ðéərfɔ̀ːr] A2	10.

diet 图 [dáɪət] A2	11.	toxin 图 [tá(:)ks(ə)n]	12.
rid 形 [ríd] B1	13.	get rid of ...	14.
besides 前 [bɪsáɪdz] B1	15.		

A 【Comprehension 1】 Fill in the blanks in Japanese.

パラグラフごとの要点を整理しよう【思考力・判断力・表現力】

1	人間と動物の（1.　　　　　）の違い。 ➡人間は一般的に（2.　　　　　）時間必要だが，動物はそれぞれ異なる。
2	コアラの食べるユーカリの葉は（3.　　　　　）が多く，（4.　　　　　）が少ない。 したがって，コアラは食物から十分なエネルギーが取れない。
3	ユーカリの葉には（5.　　　）があり，ほかの動物には取り除くのが難しい。 コアラは（5.　　　）を取り除くのに多くのエネルギーを使うため，食べることや （6.　　　　　）こと以外，何もせずにエネルギーを節約する。

B 【Comprehension 2】 Answer the following questions in English.

本文のポイントについて答えよう【思考力・判断力・表現力】

1. How much of our whole life do we spend sleeping?

   ---

2. Why don't koalas get enough energy from their diet?

   ---

3. What do eucalyptus leaves contain besides water and a little nutrition?

C 【Key Sentences】 Translate the following sentences.

重要文について確認しよう【知識・技能】【思考力・判断力・表現力】

④ This means that we **spend** about one third of our whole life **sleeping**.

◆that-節が S＋V＋O の O（目的語）として用いられている。

◆〈spend＋O＋〜ing〉「〜して O を過ごす」の意味の，現在分詞を使った表現。

訳：

---

⑫ Eucalyptus leaves also contain toxins (that are hard **for other animals** to remove).

◆関係代名詞 that は先行詞が人・物・事などの区別なく使える。

◆to remove は形容詞 hard の示す範囲を限定する副詞用法。for other animals は意味上の主語を示す。

訳：

Part 3 教科書 p.25 🔊意味のまとまりに注意して，本文全体を聞こう。 ◎1-16

④ ①In contrast to koalas, / giraffes sleep / only for short periods of time. // ②Modern research shows / that giraffes usually sleep / only about two hours / a day / in total. // ③They mostly stand / while sleeping, / and they lie down / on the ground / to sleep / for only a few minutes. // ④Giraffes are the tallest land animals, / and they need to eat / a huge amount of leaves / every day / to maintain / their large bodies. // ⑤They have to spend / far more time feeding / than sleeping. //

⑤ ⑥Most large grazing mammals, / such as giraffes, / horses / and elephants, / are short-sleepers. // ⑦It takes many hours / for these animals / to eat a lot of leaves / or grass. // ⑧It is thought / that they evolved into short-sleepers / because they needed / to reduce the danger / of being attacked / by predators / like lions, / leopards / and hyenas. //

⑥ ⑨Meat-eating animals, / on the other hand, / sleep as much as / 13 to 15 hours / a day. // ⑩Their food contains / lots of protein, / so / it is very nutritious. // ⑪Therefore, / they don't have to spend / a great amount of time / feeding. //

🔊意味のまとまりに注意して，本文全体を音読しよう。(170 Words)

Words and Phrases 新出単語・表現の意味を調べよう			
contrast 名 [ká(:)ntræst] A2	1.	in contrast to …	2.
modern 形 [má(:)dərn] A2	3.	in total	4.
maintain 動 [meɪntéɪn] B1	5.	grazing 形 [gréɪzɪŋ]	6.
mammal 名 [mǽm(ə)l]	7.	sleeper 名 [slíːpər]	8.
evolve into …	9.	predator 名 [prédətər]	10.
leopard 名 [lépərd] B2	11.	hyena 名 [haɪíːnə]	12.
as much as …	13.	protein 名 [próutiːn]	14.
nutritious 形 [njuːtríʃəs] B1	15.		

A 【**Comprehension 1**】 Fill in the blanks in Japanese.

パラグラフごとの要点を整理しよう【思考力・判断力・表現力】

4	ほとんど（1.　　　　　）まま眠るキリンは，眠るより食べることに多くの時間を費やす。	[理由]
		大きな体を（2.　　　　　）するため。
5	キリンなどの大型の（3.　　　　　）の多くが短時間の睡眠である。	[理由]
		（4.　　　　　）に襲われる危険を減らす必要があるため。
6	（4.　　　　　）は長時間の睡眠である。彼らは食事の時間を多く取る必要がない。	[理由]
		彼らの食べ物は多くの（5.　　　　　）を含んでいるため。

B 【**Comprehension 2**】 Answer the following questions in English.

本文のポイントについて答えよう【思考力・判断力・表現力】

1. What does modern research about giraffes' sleep show?

　---

2. Why did most large grazing mammals evolve into short-sleepers?

　---

3. How many hours do meat-eating animals sleep a day?

C 【**Key Sentences**】 Fill in the blanks and translate the following sentences.

重要文について確認しよう【知識・技能】【思考力・判断力・表現力】

③ They mostly stand **while sleeping**, and they lie down on the ground to sleep for only a few minutes.

　◆while に導かれる副詞節中で省略が起きている。省略されている語は while（1.

　[英語2語で]） sleeping。

　訳：---

⑥ Most large grazing mammals, **such as** giraffes, horses and elephants, are short-sleepers.

　◆such as ... 「…のような〜」で，grazing mammals の例を示している。

　◆grazing は難しい単語だが，後に続く例で意味を推測することができる。

　訳：---

⑨ Meat-eating animals, **on the other hand,** sleep as much as 13 to 15 hours a day.

　◆コンマやダッシュで区切られて文の途中で説明的な役割をする挿入句が入ることがある。on the other hand は（2.　　　　[日本語で]）の意味。

　訳：---

Part 4 教科書 p.28 ◁意味のまとまりに注意して，本文全体を聞こう。 ◉1-18

7 ①Some marine mammals, / such as whales and dolphins, / have different sleeping styles. // ②They have to come regularly / up to the surface / of the sea / to breathe. // ③It is impossible / for them / to sleep / with both their brains and their bodies resting / entirely. // ④They have to keep / swimming and breathing / while sleeping. //

8 ⑤Dolphins are unique / in that / they keep one brain hemisphere / in slow-wave activity / while they sleep. // ⑥During slow-wave activity, / the hemispheres of a dolphin's brain / sleep alternately, / and they each sleep / for only a short time. // ⑦The left hemisphere / is sleeping / while the right eye is closed. // ⑧Similarly, / the right hemisphere / is inactive / while the left eye is closed. // ⑨The dolphins repeat this behavior / countless times / while they are sleeping. //

9 ⑩Affected by their living environments, / all animals / on the globe / have developed / different sleep behaviors / and different sleeping hours. // ⑪Their lifestyles are / the results of evolution / and specialization. // ⑫Research on animal sleep / has made many interesting facts / clear to us. //

◁意味のまとまりに注意して，本文全体を音読しよう。（161 Words）

Words and Phrases 新出単語・表現の意味を調べよう			
marine 形 [mərí:n] B1	1.	regularly 副 [régjələrli] A2	2.
breathe 動 [brí:ð] A2	3.	impossible 形 [ɪmpá(:)səb(ə)l] A2	4.
entirely 副 [ɪntáɪərli] B1	5.	in that …	6.
hemisphere 名 [hémɪsfɪər]	7.	alternately 副 [ɔ́:ltərnətli]	8.
similarly 副 [sím(ə)lərli] B1	9.	inactive 形 [ɪnǽktɪv]	10.
behavior 名 [bɪhéɪvjər] A2	11.	countless 形 [káʊntləs] B1	12.
affect 動 [əfékt] B1	13.	globe 名 [ɡlóʊb] A2	14.
specialization 名 [spèʃ(ə)ləzéɪʃ(ə)n]	15.		

A 【Comprehension 1】 Fill in the blanks in Japanese.

パラグラフごとの要点を整理しよう【思考力・判断力・表現力】

7	(₁.　　　　　　　) の眠りのスタイル 定期的に海水面へ出て（₂.　　　　　　　） をする → 眠っている間も泳ぎ続ける。
8	イルカの眠りのスタイル 片方ずつ（₃.　　　　） を休ませる。 ・(₄.　　　　　　　) が閉じている→左の（₃.　　　　） が休んでいる。 ・(₅.　　　　　　　) が閉じている→右の（₃.　　　　） が休んでいる。
9	(₆.　　　　　　　) の影響を受けて，地球上のすべての動物は，さまざまな（₇.　　　　　　　　） や睡眠時間を発達させてきた。

B 【Comprehension 2】 Answer the following questions in English.

本文のポイントについて答えよう【思考力・判断力・表現力】

1. Why do some marine mammals have to come regularly up to the surface of the sea?

　...

2. What is a unique point of how dolphins sleep?

　...

3. What research has made many interesting facts clear to us?

　...

C 【Key Sentences】 Fill in the blanks and translate the following sentences.

重要文について確認しよう【知識・技能】【思考力・判断力・表現力】

③ **It is** impossible for them **to** sleep **with** both their brains and their bodies **resting** entirely.

　◆It は形式主語で to-不定詞以降が真主語。意味上の主語は（₁.　　　　　　[日本語で]）。

　◆〈with＋O＋分詞〉で主節の出来事との同時的「つながり」である付帯状況を表す。with both their brains and their bodies resting entirely「脳も身体もすっかり休んだままで」。

　訳:...

④ They have to keep swimming and breathing **while sleeping**.

　◆省略されている語は while（₂.　　　　　[英語 2 語で]） sleeping。

　訳:...

⑩ **Affected by their living environments,** all animals on the globe have developed different sleep behaviors and different sleeping hours.

　◆affected by ... 「…に影響を受けて」受け身の分詞構文。

　訳:...

Activity Plus 　教科書 p.32〜p.33　◁意味のまとまりに注意して，本文全体を聞こう。　◎1-20

①A Japanese high school student asks some questions / of an expert / who studies human sleep. // ②The expert answers the student, / showing graphs. //

Student: ③Do you think / Japanese people generally get / enough sleep? //

　Expert: ④According to a recent survey, / the average sleeping time / of Japanese adults / is getting shorter. // ⑤As Graph 1 shows, / the number of people / who sleep less than six hours / every day / has been increasing, / and the number of people / getting more than seven hours of sleep / has been decreasing. //

Student: ⑥What's the purpose of sleep? // ⑦What is important / about sleep? //

　Expert: ⑧Sleep helps us / get rid of our fatigue. // ⑨It is also important / for refreshing our brain / and keeping it healthy. // ⑩A shortage of sleep is bad / for our health, / and it increases / our risk of obesity / and heart disease. // ⑪Eventually, / it raises our risk of death. //

Student: ⑫Is it better / for us / to sleep as long as we can / to stay healthy? //

　Expert: ⑬Sleeping too long / may not be better / for us. // ⑭One interesting fact / we have learned from studies is / that those who sleep longer / than eight hours / a day / have a higher risk of death, / too, / like short-sleepers. // ⑮Graph 2 shows / that people who sleep / around seven hours / a day / have the lowest risk of death. //

◁意味のまとまりに注意して，本文全体を音読しよう。（206 Words）

Words and Phrases 新出単語・表現の意味を調べよう			
ask A of B	1.	expert 名 [ékspəːrt] A2	2.
generally 副 [dʒén(ə)r(ə)li] B1	3.	recent 形 [ríːs(ə)nt] A2	4.
average 形 [ǽv(ə)rɪdʒ] A2	5.	less than ...	6.
fatigue 名 [fətíːg]	7.	refresh 動 [rɪfréʃ]	8.
shortage 名 [ʃɔ́ːrtɪdʒ] B1	9.	obesity 名 [oʊbíːsəti]	10.
male 名 [méɪl] A2	11.		

22

A 【**Comprehension 1**】 Fill in the blanks in Japanese.

日本の成人の平均睡眠時間
［グラフ 1 ］ 最近の調査では，睡眠時間が 6 時間未満の人は（1. ） いる。 また，7 時間以上の睡眠時間の人は（2. ） いる。
睡眠の役割
（3. ） を取り除く。（4. ） を回復させ，健康に保つ。 睡眠不足だと，（5. ） や心臓病の危険性が増える。
長すぎる睡眠時間の影響
［グラフ 2 ］ およそ 7 時間睡眠をとる人は（6. ） の危険性が最も低い。

B 【**Comprehension 2**】 Answer the following questions in English.

1. How is the average sleeping time of Japanese adults changing?

-----

2. According to Graph 2, who has the lowest risk of death?

C 【**Key Sentences**】 Fill in the blank and translate the following sentences.

② The expert answers the student, **showing** graphs.

◆分詞に導かれる句が副詞のように文の内容を補足説明している分詞構文。ここでは「同時」を意味する。

訳： -----

⑤ As Graph 1 shows, the number of people (**who** sleep less than six hours every day) has been increasing, and the number of people (**getting** more than seven hours of sleep) has been decreasing.

◆the number of people … every day が前半の文の主部。関係代名詞 who 以下が people を修飾している。

◆後半の people を修飾する現在分詞 getting は more than seven hours of sleep という目的語をともなうため修飾する名詞の後ろに付く。

訳： -----

⑭ One interesting fact we have learned from studies is that **those who** sleep longer than eight hours a day have a higher risk of death, too, like short-sleepers.

◆one interesting fact と we have learned の間には関係代名詞の目的格の省略が起きている。

◆補語になる that-節中の動詞は（1. ［英語で］）

◆ those who … で「…（する）人々」の意味。

訳： -----

Part 1 教科書 p.38〜p.39 ◁意味のまとまりに注意して，本文全体を聞こう。 ◎1-22

①You found / two short video clips / of tennis player / Naomi Osaka's victory speeches / on the Internet. // ②You are watching them. //

A

③Naomi's speech / after her final match / against Serena Williams / (USA) / in the 2018 U.S. Open Championships //

④I know / that everyone was cheering / for Serena Williams, / and I'm sorry / our final match / had to end / like this. // ⑤I'd just like to / thank all of you / for coming / and watching / this match. //

⑥It was always my dream / to play with Serena / in the U.S. Open finals. // ⑦So / I'm glad / that I was able to / do that, / and I'm grateful / I was able to / play with her. // ⑧Thank you! //

B

⑨Naomi's speech / after her final match / against Petra Kvitová / (the Czech Republic) / in the 2019 Australian Open Championships //

⑩Huge congrats / to you, / Petra, / and your team! // ⑪I've always wanted / to play with you. // ⑫And you've been through / hardships. // ⑬You're really amazing. // ⑭I was honored / to play with you / in the final. //

⑮Even though it's very hot, / many people still came / to show support, / so I want / to show my gratitude / to them, / too. // ⑯So, / thanks to Craig, / the tournament director, / the ball kids / running around / in the heat, / the umpires, / the volunteers, / everyone. // ⑰They make this tournament possible, / so I want / to thank them all, / too. // ⑱And thanks / to my team. // ⑲There is always a team / behind a tennis player. //

◁意味のまとまりに注意して，本文全体を音読しよう。（228 Words）

Words and Phrases	新出単語・表現の意味を調べよう		
clip 图[klíp] B1	1.	victory 图[víkt(ə)ri] B1	2.
Serena Williams [səríːnə wíljəmz]	セリーナ・ウィリアムズ	cheer for …	3.
grateful 形[gréɪtf(ə)l] A2	4.	Petra Kvitová [pétrə kvítəvə]	ペトラ・クビトバ
Czech Republic 图 [tʃék rɪpʌ́blɪk]	5.	congrats 閪[kəngrǽts]	6.

gratitude 名 [grǽtətjùːd] B1	7.	Craig [kréɪɡ]	クレイグ
umpire 名[ʌ́mpaɪər]	8.		

A 【Comprehension 1】 Fill in the blanks in Japanese.

要点を整理しよう【思考力・判断力・表現力】

試合した年と対戦相手	大坂選手のスピーチ内容
2018年 セリーナ・ウィリアムズ	みんなが（1.　　　　　　　　　　　　）を応援していたのを知っていたので謝った。全米オープンの（2.　　　　　　　　）でセリーナと対戦することが夢であった。
（3.　　　　　　）年 ペトラ・クビトバ	ペトラが本当にすばらしいと称え，トーナメントに関わったすべての人への（4.　　　　）を述べている。

B 【Comprehension 2】 Answer the following questions in English.

本文のポイントについて答えよう【思考力・判断力・表現力】

1. Why did Naomi say "I'm sorry our final match had to end like this"?

....

2. How was the weather on the day of the final match of the 2019 Australian Open Championships?

....

3. According to Naomi, what is always behind a tennis player?

....

C 【Key Sentences】 Fill in the blanks and translate the following sentences.

重要文について確認しよう【知識・技能】【思考力・判断力・表現力】

⑦ **I'm glad that** I was able to do **that**.

◆ be glad that … は「…してうれしい」の意味。形容詞が，that-節が表す場面や状況に対する主語の感情や態度を表す。

◆文末の that ＝（1.　　　　　　　　　　　　　[日本語で]）。

訳：..

⑰ **They** make this tournament possible, so I want to thank **them**.

（O = this tournament, C = possible）

◆ make＋O＋C「O を C にする」の文型。

◆ They, them ＝（2.　　　　　　　　　　　　[日本語で]）。

◆ this tournament ＝（3.　　　　　　　　[日本語で]）。

訳：..

Part 2 教科書 p.40 🔈意味のまとまりに注意して，本文全体を聞こう。 ◎1-24

①Professional athletes / around the world / often make a victory speech / in English. // ②Their speeches have / some features / in common. // ③What are they? //

① ④What do athletes tell people / in their victory speeches / after the competition is over? // ⑤You can find / four features / in their speeches / that attract people. // ⑥They are: / to honor their opponents, / to acknowledge their opponents' achievements, / to express their sincere thanks, / and to show humility. // ⑦Let's check each feature / one by one. //

② ⑧First, / it is important / for athletes / to praise their opponents / at the beginning / of their speeches. // ⑨They usually keep eye contact / with their opponents. // ⑩For example, / Naomi Osaka, / who won the final match / of the 2018 U.S. Open Championships, / sincerely honored her opponent, / Serena Williams. // ⑪Serena also did that / in her speech. // ⑫It doesn't matter / whether they win / or lose. //

③ ⑬Second, / many winners acknowledge / their opponents' hard work. // ⑭Their opponents probably / had to overcome / some difficulties / before the tournament, / such as injuries, / slumps / or frustrations. // ⑮For example, / in the 2019 Australian Open Championships, / Naomi said to her opponent, / Petra Kvitová, / "You've been through hardships." //

🔈意味のまとまりに注意して，本文全体を音読しよう。（178 Words）

Words and Phrases 新出単語・表現の意味を調べよう			
attract 動 [ətrǽkt] B1	1.	opponent 名 [əpóunənt] B2	2.
acknowledge 動 [əkná(:)lɪdʒ] B1	3.	sincere 形 [sɪnsíər] B2	4.
humility 名 [hjuːmíləti]	5.	one by one	6.
praise 動 [préɪz] B2	7.	at the beginning of …	8.
sincerely 副 [sɪnsíərli]	9.	whether 接 [(h)wéðər] B1	10.
probably 副 [prá(:)bəbli] A2	11.	overcome 動 [òuvərkÁm] B1	12.
injury 名 [ín(d)ʒ(ə)ri] B1	13.	slump 名 [slÁmp]	14.

A 【**Comprehension 1**】 Fill in the blanks in Japanese.

パラグラフごとの要点を整理しよう【思考力・判断力・表現力】

スポーツ選手のスピーチの4つの特徴	具体例
1．スピーチの (1.　　　　　　) に対戦相手をほめる。	大坂なおみ選手は2018年全米オープンの決勝戦で，勝利した相手であるセリーナ・ウィリアムズ選手を称えた。セリーナ選手も同様に大坂選手を称えた。 ➡(2.　　　　　　) は関係ない。
2．対戦相手がけがやスランプのような (3.　　　　　　) を乗り越えてきたことを認める。	(4.　　　　　　) 年の全豪オープンで，大坂選手は対戦相手のペトラ・クビトバ選手が (3.　　　　　　) を乗り越えてきたことを認めた。
3．心からの感謝を表す。	
4．謙遜を示す。	

B 【**Comprehension 2**】 Answer the following questions in English.

本文のポイントについて答えよう【思考力・判断力・表現力】

1. When do athletes usually praise their opponents in their speeches?

   ----

2. What are some examples of athletes' hardships?

C 【**Key Sentences**】 Fill in the blanks and translate the following sentences.

重要文について確認しよう【知識・技能】【思考力・判断力・表現力】

⑧ **First**, **it** is important for athletes to praise their opponents at the beginning of their speeches.

   ◆ First は列挙のディスコースマーカーで，(1.　　　　　　　　　　　　　　　[日本語で]) の最初の例を示している。
   ◆ it は形式主語で，真主語は to praise their opponents at the beginning of their speeches.
   訳 : --

⑩ Naomi Osaka (**, who** won the final match of the 2018 U.S. Open Championships), sincerely honored her opponent, Serena Williams.

   ◆ , who は関係代名詞の非制限用法。大坂選手の補足説明をする節が続く。
   ◆ この文の主節の動詞は (2.　　　　　　　　[英語で])。
   ◆ her opponent と Serena Williams は同格。
   訳 : --

⑫ **It** doesn't matter **whether** they win **or** lose.

   ◆ whether A or B は「A であろうが B であろうが」の意味。形式主語 It の真主語となっている。
   訳 : --

Part 3 教科書 p.41 ◁意味のまとまりに注意して，本文全体を聞こう。 ◎1-26

4 ①Third, / players often thank / all of their fans / and supporters. // ②There are always coaches, / teammates, / trainers, / managers and nutritionists / behind a professional athlete. // ③They are all working together / as a team. // ④Besides them, / many staff members, / such as judges, / officials, / sponsors and ball kids, / are essential / to organize a tournament. // ⑤If these people did not support athletes, / there couldn't be a tournament. //

5 ⑥In the 2019 Rugby World Cup / in Japan, / South Africa defeated England / in the final game. // ⑦Siya Kolisi, / who was the captain, / expressed his gratitude / to his own country, / South Africa, / in his victory interview. // ⑧He said to people / in his country, / "I cannot thank you enough. // ⑨I'm so grateful / to all the people / in South Africa / for cheering for us." //

6 ⑩The baseball player / Shohei Otani / was named Rookie of the Year / in 2018. // ⑪In his speech / at the awards ceremony, / he thanked all the people / concerned with the award / he received. // ⑫They were the people / hosting the great event, / the baseball writers voting for him, / the entire Angels organization, / his fans, / and his parents. //

◁意味のまとまりに注意して，本文全体を音読しよう。（177 Words）

Words and Phrases 新出単語・表現の意味を調べよう			
nutritionist 名 [nju:tríʃ(ə)nəst]	1.	staff 名 [stæf] A2	2.
sponsor 名 [spá(:)nsər] B1	3.	organize 動 [ɔ́:rgənàɪz] A2	4.
defeat 動 [dɪfí:t] B1	5.	Siya Kolisi [síːjə koulíːsi]	シヤ・コリシ
be grateful to A for B	6.	rookie 名 [rúki]	7.
award 名 [əwɔ́:rd] A2	8.	ceremony 名 [sérəmòuni] B1	9.
concerned 形 [kənsə́:rnd] B1	10.	be concerned with …	11.
vote for …	12.	entire 形 [ɪntáɪər] B1	13.
Angels [éɪn(d)ʒ(ə)lz]	エンゼルス	organization 名 [ɔ̀:rg(ə)nəzéɪʃ(ə)n] B1	14.

A 【**Comprehension 1**】 Fill in the blanks in Japanese.

パラグラフごとの要点を整理しよう【思考力・判断力・表現力】

スポーツ選手のスピーチの4つの特徴	具体例
1．対戦相手をほめる。	
2．対戦相手の業績を認める。	
3．ファンやサポーターに （1.　　　　　）を表す。 ➡支えてくれる人がいなければ大 　会はできない。	2019年　シヤ・コリシ選手 ワールドカップ優勝のインタビューで（2.　　　　）に 対しての感謝を表現した。 （3.　　　　　）年　大谷翔平選手 セレモニーで（4.　　　　）の受賞に関わったすべて の人に感謝した。
4．謙遜を示す。	

B 【**Comprehension 2**】 Answer the following questions in English.

本文のポイントについて答えよう【思考力・判断力・表現力】

1. Who are essential for organizing a tournament?

----

2. What country won the 2019 Rugby World Cup?

----

3. Who was named the MLB Rookie of the Year in 2018?

C 【**Key Sentences**】 Fill in the blank and translate the following sentences.

重要文について確認しよう【知識・技能】【思考力・判断力・表現力】

⑤ **If** these people **did not support** athletes, there **couldn't be** a tournament.

◆〈If＋S＋動詞の過去形 …, S＋could 〜〉は仮定法過去で，現在の事実に反することを仮定する。

訳:--

⑦ Siya Kolisi (**, who** was the captain), expressed his gratitude to his own country, South Africa, in his victory interview.

◆, who は関係代名詞の非制限用法。シヤ・コリシ選手の補足説明をする節を挿入する。

◆この文の主節の動詞は（1.　　　　　[英語で]）。

訳:--

⑪ He thanked all the people (concerned with the award he received).

◆concerned は形容詞［過去分詞］で，直前の all the people を修飾。

◆the award と he received の間に関係代名詞 that（which）が省略されている。

訳:--

29

Part 4 教科書 p.42 🔊意味のまとまりに注意して，本文全体を聞こう。 ◎1-28

7 ①Finally, / showing humility / is a technique / quite unique to the speeches / of professional athletes. // ②They intentionally confess / their worries or weaknesses / in their speeches, / which hurts no one / and makes a favorable impression / on listeners. // ③Being humble / can be difficult, / but athletes often use / this technique / in their speeches. //

8 ④At the awards ceremony / for Rookie of the Year, / Shohei Otani was holding / his notes for his speech. // ⑤He looked down at them frequently / during his speech. // ⑥However, / he finished his speech / with the sentence, / "Hopefully, / I will not need this cheat sheet / the next time I'm up here." // ⑦Showing humility / made his audience laugh / at just the right time. //

9 ⑧You can learn / what professional athletes think / by looking at these four special features / in their victory speeches. // ⑨When you deliver a speech / in English, / you can use some of these techniques / to make your speech / more impressive. // ⑩If you analyze / athletes' outstanding speeches, / you too can become a speaker / who is attractive / to your audience. //

🔊意味のまとまりに注意して，本文全体を音読しよう。 (165 Words)

Words and Phrases	新出単語・表現の意味を調べよう		
technique 名 [tekníːk] B1	1.	intentionally 副 [ɪnténʃ(ə)n(ə)li] B1	2.
confess 動 [kənfés] B2	3.	weakness 名 [wíːknəs] B1	4.
favorable 形 [féɪv(ə)rəb(ə)l] B1	5.	impression 名 [ɪmpréʃ(ə)n] B1	6.
make an impression on …	7.	humble 形 [hámb(ə)l] B2	8.
frequently 副 [fríːkwəntli] B1	9.	finish A with B	10.
hopefully 副 [hóʊpf(ə)li] B1	11.	cheat 名 [tʃíːt]	12.
the next time	13.	audience 名 [ɔ́ːdiəns] A2	14.
at the right time	15.	impressive 形 [ɪmprésɪv] B1	16.

analyze 動 [ǽnəlàɪz] B1	17.	outstanding 形 [àʊtstǽndɪŋ] B1	18.
be attractive to …	19.		

A 【**Comprehension 1**】 Fill in the blanks in Japanese.

パラグラフごとの要点を整理しよう【思考力・判断力・表現力】

スポーツ選手のスピーチの 4 つの特徴	具体例
1．対戦相手をほめる。	
2．対戦相手の業績を認める。	
3．心からの感謝を表す。	
4．（1.　　　　　）を示す。 ➡意図的に悩みや弱点を （2.　　　　　）する。	2018年　大谷翔平選手 スピーチで（3.　　　　　）を持って下を見て話していたが，次回はできれば（3.　　　　　）が不要になればよいと述べ，観客を笑わせた。

B 【**Comprehension 2**】 Answer the following questions in English.

本文のポイントについて答えよう【思考力・判断力・表現力】

1. In athletes' speech, what may make a favorable impression on listeners?

---

2. What does Shohei want to stop using when he makes another speech?

---

3. Why did Shohei's audience laugh at the awards ceremony for Rookie of the Year?

C 【**Key Sentences**】 Fill in the blanks and translate the following sentences.

重要文について確認しよう【知識・技能】【思考力・判断力・表現力】

② They intentionally confess their worries or weaknesses in their speeches, **which** hurts no one and makes a favorable impression on listeners.

◆非制限用法の関係代名詞 which は，前に述べられた節全体を先行詞とする場合がある。
　この文の先行詞は（1.　　　　　　　　　　　[日本語で]）ということ。
◆ They＝（2.　　　　　[英語 2 語で]）
訳 :

---

⑩ **If** you analyze athletes' outstanding speeches, you **too** can become a speaker (who is attractive to your audience).

◆この文の If は条件を表す接続詞で，続く文は仮定法にはなっていない。実際に読者がスポーツ選手のスピーチを分析する可能性が十分にあることを想定している。
◆ too は「スポーツ選手だけでなくあなた自身も魅力的なスピーチができる」の意味で使われている。
訳 :

31

Activity Plus 教科書 p.48~p.49 ◁意味のまとまりに注意して，本文全体を聞こう。 ◎1-30

①You found a victory speech / by the tennis player / Roger Federer / on the Internet. // ②You are listening to it. //

③Roger's speech / after his final match / against Marin Cilic / (Croatia) / in the 2017 Wimbledon Championships //

④Marin Cilic / is a hero. // ⑤Congratulations / on his running second. // ⑥He played perfectly / in the final, / but it was a bad result / for him. // ⑦I really hope / there will be another good result / for him / in the future. //

⑧I can't believe / I was able to win / without losing any sets. // ⑨There were times / when I couldn't believe / I could take part in the final. // ⑩However, / I decided / to believe it. // ⑪And Marin and I did it! // ⑫It was a great time / to be able to compete / with Marin here / today. // ⑬The center court / was filled with a lot of spectators / and had a great atmosphere. // ⑭I will be back here / again / next year. //

⑮My little sons, / watching from their seats, / don't know what's going on. // ⑯They might think / this place is a good playground. // ⑰My daughters understand this situation / a little, / but I will have to talk to them / about this / again. // ⑱I'm so grateful / to my family / for supporting me! // ⑲I couldn't have played / in such a wonderful match / if I hadn't had / your great support. // ⑳Thank you again / very much. //

◁意味のまとまりに注意して，本文全体を音読しよう。(216 Words)

Words and Phrases 新出単語・表現の意味を調べよう			
Roger Federer [rá(:)dʒər fédərər]	ロジャー・フェデラー	Marin Cilic [mǽrin tʃíliʧ]	マリン・チリッチ
Croatia 名 [krouéɪʃə]	1.	Wimbledon [wímb(ə)ld(ə)n]	ウィンブルドン
congratulation 間 [kəngrǽtʃəléɪʃ(ə)n]	2.	compete 動 [kəmpíːt] B1	3.
spectator 名 [spéktèɪtər] B1	4.	atmosphere 名 [ǽtməsfìər] B1	5.
go on	6.		

A 【**Comprehension 1**】 Fill in the blanks in Japanese.

2017年ウィンブルドン決勝を勝ち抜いたロジャー・フェデラー選手のスピーチ	
【スピーチの冒頭】 1．（1.　　　　　）をほめる。	マリン・チリッチ選手は（2.　　　　　）である。 決勝では（3.　　　　　）なプレーをした。 今回は残念な結果であったが，将来，チリッチ選手は よい結果を残すことができることを本当に望んでいる。
【展開】	決勝戦に行けるかどうか不安なこともあった。 チリッチ選手とその日センターコートで戦えたことは すばらしい時間であった。 満員のセンターコートの雰囲気はすばらしいものであ り，来年も帰ってくるつもりだ。
【締めくくり】 3．心からの（4.　　　　　）を表す。	支えてくれた（5.　　　　　）に感謝した。

B 【**Comprehension 2**】 Answer the following questions in English.

1. Who won the 2017 Wimbledon Championships, Roger or Marin?

   ....

2. How many sets did Roger lose during the Championships?

   ....

3. Who did Roger thank in his speech?

   ....

C 【**Key Sentences**】 Fill in the blank and translate the following sentences.

⑨ There were <u>times</u> (**when** I couldn't believe I could **take part in** the final).

　◆関係副詞 when は，先行詞が時を表す場合に使われる。

　◆ take part in ... は「…に（1.　　　　　[日本語で]）」の意味。

　訳： ....

⑮ My little sons, **watching** from their seats, don't know **what's going on**.

　◆ watching は分詞構文で，主節の動詞と同時であることを付帯状況的に示している。

　◆ what's going on は名詞句で，「何が起こっているのか」の意味。

　訳： ....

⑲ I **couldn't have played** in such a wonderful match **if** I **hadn't had** your great support.

　◆仮定法過去完了で，過去の事実に反することを仮定する。

　訳： ....

Part 1 教科書 p.54〜p.55 ◀意味のまとまりに注意して，本文全体を聞こう。◎1-32

①You join an international event / about disaster prevention. // ②You find a poster. //

③There Are More Disasters / These Days! //

④We often hear sad news / about heavy rains, / typhoons / and earthquakes. // ⑤They are constantly happening / all over the world. // ⑥People are suffering. // ⑦Their houses are destroyed. // ⑧They have nowhere to go. // ⑨"They" may be "you" / tomorrow. //

⑩The graph shows / how many natural disasters have been reported / around the world / since 1990. // ⑪It may be true / that past disasters are underreported. // ⑫However, / it seems / that the number has increased / recently. // ⑬Some researchers suggest / that climate change has something to do / with this increase. //

⑭Typical examples of natural disasters include floods, / droughts, / storms, / volcanic eruptions / and earthquakes. // ⑮They have caused the deaths of millions of people / as well as huge economic losses. // ⑯What can we do / to deal with these disasters? // ⑰Now is the time / to act seriously / on this global issue. //

◀意味のまとまりに注意して，本文全体を音読しよう。(148 Words)

Words and Phrases 新出単語・表現の意味を調べよう			
disaster 名[dɪzǽstər] B1	1.	prevention 名 [prɪvénʃ(ə)n] B2	2.
typhoon 名[taɪfúːn]	3.	constantly 副 [ká(ː)nst(ə)ntli] B1	4.
nowhere 副 [nóʊ(h)wèər] B1	5.	underreport 動 [ʌ̀ndərrɪpɔ́ːrt]	6.
recently 副[ríːs(ə)ntli] A2	7.	researcher 名 [rɪsə́ːrtʃər] B1	8.
suggest 動[sə(g)dʒést] A2	9.	have something to do with …	10.
drought 名[dráʊt] B2	11.	volcanic 形[vɑ(ː)lkǽnɪk]	12.
eruption 名[ɪrʌ́pʃ(ə)n] B2	13.	loss 名[lɔ́ːs] B1	14.
act on …	15.		

A 【Comprehension 1】 Fill in the blanks in Japanese.

被害を受けるのは明日の「あなた」かもしれない。

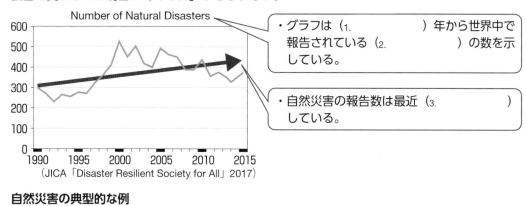

Number of Natural Disasters

(JICA「Disaster Resilient Society for All」2017)

・グラフは（1.　　　　　）年から世界中で報告されている（2.　　　　　）の数を示している。

・自然災害の報告数は最近（3.　　　　　）している。

自然災害の典型的な例

・洪水　　　・(4.　　　　　)　　　・暴風雨　　　・火山の(5.　　　　　)　　　・地震

B 【Comprehension 2】 Answer the following questions in English.

1. What are three examples of sad news we often hear?

   ----

2. According to some researchers, what has something to do with the increase in the number of natural disasters?

   ----

3. Other than the deaths of many people, what have natural disasters caused?

C 【Key Sentences】 Translate the following sentences.

⑩ The graph shows <u>how many natural disasters have been reported around the world since 1990.</u>
　　　　　　　　　　　　　　　　　　　　　　　　　　　　O
　◆〈疑問詞＋S＋V〉で名詞節。ここでは how many natural disasters が節内の主語の働きをする。
　訳：--

⑪ **It** may be true <u>that past disasters are underreported.</u>
　◆It は that-節を真主語とする形式主語。
　訳：--

⑰ **Now is the time to** act seriously on this global issue.
　◆Now is the time to ～「今こそ～するときだ」。to-不定詞は the time を修飾する。
　訳：--

Part 2 　教科書 p.56 　🔊意味のまとまりに注意して，本文全体を聞こう。 ◉1-34

①More and more natural disasters / seem to be happening / around the world. //

②Are you well prepared / to reduce your own risk / from future disasters? //

[1] ③Different regions in the world / have unique types of natural disasters. // ④Africa tends to suffer / from droughts. // ⑤In Latin America, / earthquakes and tsunamis occur / frequently. // ⑥Asia is likely / to suffer damage / from floods / and storms. //

[2] ⑦Japan is known / to have suffered from natural disasters / frequently / and severely. // ⑧Earthquakes and typhoons / in particular / have affected our lives. // ⑨Earthquakes in Japan / account for about 20 percent / of the world's occurrences / with a magnitude of six / or higher. // ⑩Typhoons bring strong winds / and heavy rains, / resulting in flooding / and landslides. // ⑪Climate change may be increasing / the risk of disasters. //

[3] ⑫Traditional approaches / to disaster prevention / and risk management / may not be enough. // ⑬We have developed infrastructure / such as roads, / buildings / and dams. // ⑭We have also trained ourselves / through evacuation drills / at school / and in communities. // ⑮Even so, / natural disasters still continue / to destroy life / and property. // ⑯What else can we do / to deal with future disasters? // 　🔊意味のまとまりに注意して，本文全体を音読しよう。（176 Words）

Words and Phrases	新出単語・表現の意味を調べよう		
region 名[rí:dʒ(ə)n] B1	1.	Latin America 名 [lǽt(ə)n əmérɪkə]	2.
occur 動[əkə́ːr] B1	3.	be likely to ～	4.
damage 名[dǽmɪdʒ] B1	5.	severely 副[sɪvíərli] B1	6.
particular 形 [pərtíkjələr] B2	7.	in particular	8.
account for …	9.	occurrence 名 [əkə́ːr(ə)ns]	10.
magnitude 名[mǽgnɪtjùːd]	11.	result in …	12.
landslide 名[lǽndslàɪd] B2	13.	management 名 [mǽnɪdʒmənt] B1	14.

infrastructure 名 [ínfrəstrʌ̀ktʃər]	15.	dam 名 [dǽm] A2	16.
evacuation 名 [ɪvæ̀kjuéɪʃ(ə)n] B2	17.	property 名 [prɑ́(:)pərti] B1	18.

A 【Comprehension 1】 Fill in the blanks in Japanese.

パラグラフごとの要点を整理しよう【思考力・判断力・表現力】

世界の自然災害の特徴：
・世界のさまざまな地域には独自の自然災害の種類がある。
　A　アフリカ：(1.　　　　　　)
　B　ラテンアメリカ：地震・津波
　C　アジア：(2.　　　　　　)・暴風雨

日本の自然災害の特徴：
・世界で起こるマグニチュード6以上の地震の約 (3.　　　) パーセントを占める。
・台風が強風と大雨をもたらし，洪水や (4.　　　　　) が起こっている。

従来の防災が問いかけるもの：
・私たちはインフラの整備や (5.　　　　　　) をしてきたが，自然災害は私たちの暮らしや財産を破壊している。
➡将来の災害に対処するために，ほかに何をすることができるか。

B 【Comprehension 2】 Answer the following questions in English.

本文のポイントについて答えよう【思考力・判断力・表現力】

1.　What is Asia likely to suffer?

2.　What are two examples of natural disasters that have affected the lives in Japan?

3.　What do natural disasters continue to do?

C 【Key Sentences】 Translate the following sentences.

重要文について確認しよう【知識・技能】【思考力・判断力・表現力】

⑦　Japan is known **to have suffered** from natural disasters frequently and severely.
◆完了不定詞は〈to have＋過去分詞〉の形で，主節の動詞が表す「時」よりも以前の内容を表す。
訳：----

⑩　Typhoons bring strong winds and heavy rains, **resulting** in flooding and landslides.
◆現在分詞 resulting で始まる句が分詞構文となっている。連続して起こる動作を表す。
訳：----

Part 3 教科書 p.58 ◀意味のまとまりに注意して，本文全体を聞こう。 ◎1-36

4 ①Recent ideas and technologies / allow us to prepare / for disasters. // ②For example, / you may have heard / about hazard maps. // ③They tell you / the nearest evacuation sites / in the areas / where disasters are likely to occur. // ④Learning about the area / where you live beforehand, / or even after a disaster has happened, / will help you avoid / potential risks / in the future. //

5 ⑤Emergency food is also gaining popularity. // ⑥Nowadays, / you can buy / a variety of foods, / such as easy-to-make rice, / pre-packaged curry / and canned bread. // ⑦They can be eaten / with little preparation / and stored / for a couple of years. // ⑧It is said / that you should store / a minimum of a three-day supply of food. // ⑨Of course, / you can eat the food / as part of your daily meals / before the food's best-before date. //

6 ⑩In addition, / you need to think / about what to do / if the power goes out. // ⑪An emergency radio / can keep you updated / with disaster information. // ⑫Some radios are rechargeable / with solar panels / or hand cranks. // ⑬You can use such a radio / not only as an emergency flashlight / but also as a battery charger / for your digital devices. // ⑭Having such a power source / will make a big difference. // ◀意味のまとまりに注意して，本文全体を音読しよう。(196 Words)

Words and Phrases 新出単語・表現の意味を調べよう			
allow ... to 〜	1.	prepare for ...	2.
hazard 名[hǽzərd] B1	3.	beforehand 副 [bɪfɔ́ːrhænd]	4.
avoid 動[əvɔ́ɪd] A2	5.	emergency 名 [ɪmə́ːrdʒ(ə)nsi] A2	6.
popularity 名 [pà(:)pjəlǽrəti] B2	7.	pre-packaged 形 [prìːpǽkɪdʒd]	8.
preparation 名 [prèpəréɪʃ(ə)n] B1	9.	minimum 名 [mínɪməm] B1	10.
go out	11.	update 動 [ʌpdéɪt] B1	12.
update A with B	13.	rechargeable 形 [rìːtʃɑ́ːrdʒəb(ə)l]	14.
crank 名 [krǽŋk]	15.	flashlight 名 [flǽʃlàɪt]	16.

| charger 名[tʃɑ́ːrdʒər] | 17. | digital 形[dídʒɪt(ə)l] B1 | 18. |

A 【Comprehension 1】 Fill in the blanks in Japanese.

パラグラフごとの要点を整理しよう【思考力・判断力・表現力】

4	防災のアイディアや技術の具体例①：ハザードマップ ・災害の起こる可能性がある地域の最寄りの（1.　　　　　　　　）を伝える。 ➡将来の潜在的な（2.　　　　　　　　）を避けることに役立つ。
5	防災のアイディアや技術の具体例②：非常食 ・さまざまな種類の食品が販売されている。 ➡わずかな準備で食べられて，数年間（3.　　　　　　）することが可能である。
6	防災のアイディアや技術の具体例③：防災ラジオ ・災害情報で自分をアップデートしておくことができる。 ・太陽光パネルや手回しハンドルによって充電できるものもある。 ➡懐中電灯やデジタル機器の（4.　　　　　　）として使うことができる。

B 【Comprehension 2】 Answer the following questions in English.

本文のポイントについて答えよう【思考力・判断力・表現力】

1. What can you do if you learn about the area where you live?

----

2. How long can emergency foods be stored?

----

3. What do some radios have for recharging their batteries?

C 【Key Sentences】 Fill in the blank and translate the following sentences.

重要文について確認しよう【知識・技能】【思考力・判断力・表現力】

② **For example**, you **may have heard** about hazard maps.
　◆ for example は「例示」のディスコースマーカー。ここでは（1.
　　　[日本語で]）の例を挙げている。
　◆ may have＋過去分詞は（2.　　　　　　　　　[日本語で]）の意味。
　訳 : ---

④ Learning about the area (**where** you live) beforehand, or even after a disaster
has happened, will help you avoid potential risks in the future.
　◆関係副詞 where を含む節が，先行詞 the area を修飾する。
　◆ help＋O＋～（＝原形不定詞）は「Oが～するのを助ける」の意味。
　訳 : ---

Part 4 教科書 p.60 ◀意味のまとまりに注意して，本文全体を聞こう。 ◉1-38

⑦ ①We should also be aware of / who is at risk / in disasters. // ②You may think of elderly people, / little children / or physically-challenged people, / but you should also think of visitors / from foreign countries. // ③Such visitors may have never experienced / an earthquake / before. // ④Some of them cannot understand Japanese. // ⑤In fact, / visitors are said to have struggled / to find proper information / in their own languages / in past earthquakes / in Japan. //

⑧ ⑥In order to help foreign people / at risk, / the use of pictograms and plain Japanese words / has gained attention / recently. // ⑦These communication tools use / illustrations and simple expressions / so that everybody can understand / their messages / easily. // ⑧Some disaster information is also available / in foreign languages, / such as English, / Chinese / and Korean, / via websites, / apps / and social media. // ⑨Such information can help everyone / in a disaster. //

⑨ ⑩Recent ideas and technologies / have improved our chances / to survive disasters. // ⑪However, / it is up to each of us / to make full use of them. // ⑫What if / a big earthquake happens / now? // ⑬What can you do / for yourself, / your family / and people around you? // ⑭It is never too early / to get prepared. //

◀意味のまとまりに注意して，本文全体を音読しよう。（186 Words）

Words and Phrases	新出単語・表現の意味を調べよう		
aware 形 [əwéər] B1	1.	be aware of ...	2.
at risk	3.	physically-challenged 形 [fízɪk(ə)litʃǽlɪn(d)ʒd]	4.
in fact	5.	struggle 動 [strʌ́g(ə)l] B2	6.
proper 形 [prɑ́(ː)pər] A2	7.	pictogram 名 [píktəgræm]	8.
plain 形 [pléɪn] B1	9.	illustration 名 [ìləstréɪʃ(ə)n] B2	10.
via 前 [váɪə] B1	11.	app 名 [ǽp]	12.
media 名 [míːdiə] B2	13.	be up to ...	14.
make use of ...	15.	what if ...?	16.

A 【Comprehension 1】 Fill in the blanks in Japanese.

パラグラフごとの要点を整理しよう【思考力・判断力・表現力】

7	さまざまな人に向けた防災への取り組みの重要性 ・災害時には，年配者，幼い子供，障害のある人たちだけではなく，日本語の理解が困難な 　(1.　　　　　　　　) からの訪問者も危険にさらされる。
8	外国人に向けた防災の取り組み事例 ・ピクトグラム・やさしい日本語：だれでもメッセージを簡単に理解できるように， 　(2.　　　　　　　　) や単純な表現を使う。 ・外国語で利用できる災害情報：ウェブサイト，(3.　　　　　　　)，(4.　　　　　　　) を通 　して提供されている。
9	災害に備えるうえでの心構え ・防災に関する最近のアイディアや技術を最大限に (5.　　　　　　　) することは，私たち 　それぞれにかかっている。

B 【Comprehension 2】 Answer the following questions in English.

本文のポイントについて答えよう【思考力・判断力・表現力】

1. What did visitors from foreign countries struggle to do in past earthquakes in Japan?

----

2. What kinds of media about disaster information are used to send messages in foreign languages?

----

3. Who should make full use of recent ideas and technologies?

C 【Key Sentences】 Fill in the blank and translate the following sentences.

重要文について確認しよう【知識・技能】【思考力・判断力・表現力】

⑤ In fact, visitors **are said to have struggled** to find proper information in their own languages in past earthquakes in Japan.

　◆S is said to ～ 「S は～すると言われている」。
　◆to have struggled は完了不定詞。struggle to ～は「～するのに苦労する」の意味。
　訳: ---

⑦ **These communication tools** use illustrations and simple expressions **so that** everybody can understand their messages easily.

　◆These communication tools＝(1.　　　　　　　　　　　　　　[英語5語で])
　◆so that S＋V は「S が V するように」の意味。
　訳: ---

①A teacher gave students the following task. // ②Koji is now making a brief presentation / about his idea. // ③After that, / Airi asks some questions. //

④TASK / What items can you create / with limited resources / in case of a disaster? // ⑤Your ideas and knowledge / will be important / in such a situation. // ⑥By using the materials below, / develop some original items / that might be useful / if you are faced / with a natural disaster. //

Koji: ⑦My idea / is to make a "cardboard bed." // ⑧In case of a disaster, / you may need / to evacuate from your home / and spend several nights / in a school gymnasium, / for example. // ⑨You can create a bed / with twelve cardboard boxes, / twelve pieces of cardboard, / and some packaging tape. // ⑩The bed can help you stay warm / during the night. // ⑪What do you think / about my idea? //

Airi: ⑫That's a great idea, / Koji. // ⑬Can the bed withstand the weight of an adult? //

Koji: ⑭Thank you / for your question. // ⑮Yes, / it can. // ⑯I forgot to tell you, / but you can put the pieces of cardboard diagonally / into each box / to reinforce the bed. //

Airi: ⑰I see. / ⑱You then seal each box / with some packaging tape, / right? //

Koji: ⑲Yes. // ⑳Just putting 12 boxes together / creates a bed. // ㉑You can also cover it / with cloth, / if you have some. //

意味のまとまりに注意して，本文全体を音読しよう。(209 Words)

Words and Phrases 新出単語・表現の意味を調べよう			
task 名[tæsk] A2	1.	brief 形[brí:f] B1	2.
resource 名[rí:sɔːrs] B1	3.	in case of …	4.
cardboard 名 [kɑ́ːrdbɔ̀ːrd] B2	5.	be faced with …	6.
foil 名[fɔ́ɪl]	7.	evacuate 動 [ɪvǽkjuèɪt] B2	8.
gymnasium 名 [dʒɪmnéɪziəm]	9.	withstand 動 [wɪðstǽnd]	10.
diagonally 副 [daɪǽg(ə)n(ə)li]	11.	reinforce 動 [rìːɪnfɔ́ːrs] B2	12.
seal 動 [síːl]	13.		

A 【**Comprehension 1**】 Fill in the blanks in Japanese.

「段ボールベッド」の作り方

［準備するもの］ (1.   ) ×12, (2.   ) ×12, (3.   )

① ② ③ ④

それぞれの
(1.   ) に
(2.   ) を
対角線に入れる。

(3.   ) で
それぞれの
(1.   ) を
ふさぐ。

12個の
(1.   ) を
くっつける。

持っている場合は,
(4.   ) でベッドを
覆う。

B 【**Comprehension 2**】 Answer the following questions in English.

本文のポイントについて答えよう【思考力・判断力・表現力】

1. What is a merit of using a cardboard bed during the night?

2. After you put the pieces of cardboard diagonally into each box, what happens?

3. What is the purpose of using some packaging tape?

C 【**Key Sentences**】 Fill in the blanks and translate the following sentences.

重要文について確認しよう【知識・技能】【思考力・判断力・表現力】

⑥ **By using** the materials below, develop some original items (**that** might be useful if you are faced with a natural disaster).

◆ by ～ing は「～することによって」の意味。
◆関係代名詞 that を含む節が, 先行詞 some original items を修飾する。
訳:

⑧ In case of a disaster, you may **need to** evacuate from your home and spend several nights in a school gymnasium, for example.

◆ need to ～に動詞の原形 (1.   [英語で]) と (2.   [英語で]) が続いている。
訳:

Part 1 教科書 p.70〜p.71 🔊意味のまとまりに注意して，本文全体を聞こう。 ◎1-42

①As a group project, / you are studying / the system of the imperial era name / in Japan. // ②On the Internet, / you found a news clip / about "Reiwa" / and some posts / about how people abroad saw / the dawn of the new era. //

③Good afternoon. // ④The name of the new era / in Japan / has just been announced. // ⑤The name of the new era / that follows Heisei / will be "Reiwa"! // ⑥The Chief Cabinet Secretary / is now holding up a white card / with the new name written / in two characters / in black ink. // ⑦"Reiwa" comes from characters / used in an introduction / to some poems / in the *Manyoshu*, / an ancient anthology / of Japanese poetry. // ⑧This introductory passage mentions / soft winds and *ume* blossoms / in spring. //

⑨What does the new name "Reiwa" / mean? //

⑩"Reiwa" is made up of two characters, / "rei" and "wa." // ⑪"Rei" can mean "beautiful" / or "good." // ⑫"Wa" can mean "harmony." // ⑬The Japanese government made an official announcement / about the English meaning of "Reiwa." // ⑭It is "the era of beautiful harmony." //

⑮Will Japan choose a beautiful harmony of peace / in the new era / of "Reiwa"? //

⑯People around the world / are now waiting to see / whether Japan will contribute / to world peace / in this new era. //

🔊意味のまとまりに注意して，本文全体を音読しよう。（200 Words）

Words and Phrases	新出単語・表現の意味を調べよう		
imperial 形 [ɪmpíəriəl]	1.	era 名 [íərə] B1	2.
dawn 名 [dɔ́:n] B2	3.	announce 動 [ənáʊns] B1	4.
chief 形 [tʃí:f] B1	5.	cabinet 名 [kǽbɪnət] B2	6.
secretary 名 [sékrətèri] A2	7.	hold up …	8.
introduction 名 [ìntrədʌ́kʃ(ə)n] B1	9.	anthology 名 [ænθá(:)lədʒi]	10.
poetry 名 [póʊətri] B1	11.	introductory 形 [ìntrədʌ́kt(ə)ri]	12.
passage 名 [pǽsɪdʒ] A2	13.	mention 動 [ménʃ(ə)n] B1	14.
blossom 名 [blá(:)s(ə)m] B2	15.	Wei [wéɪ]	ウェイ

A 【**Comprehension 1**】 Fill in the blanks in Japanese.

要点を整理しよう【思考力・判断力・表現力】

グループプロジェクト	日本の（1.　　　　　　　）の制度を研究している。
ニュースの切り抜き	新しい（1.　　　　　　）は「令和」 ➡日本和歌の古代の作品集である「（2.　　　　　）」の中の，いくつかの和歌の序文に使用されている文字に由来。
「令」の意味	「美しい」や「（3.　　　　　）」
「和」の意味	「（4.　　　　　）」

B 【**Comprehension 2**】 Answer the following questions in English.

本文のポイントについて答えよう【思考力・判断力・表現力】

1. What are you studying as a group project?

　---

2. What is the *Manyoshu*?

　---

3. According to the official announcement by the Japanese government, what is the English meaning of "Reiwa"?

C 【**Key Sentences**】 Fill in the blanks and translate the following sentences.

重要文について確認しよう【知識・技能】【思考力・判断力・表現力】

⑥ The Chief Cabinet Secretary is now holding up a white card with the new name written **in** two characters **in** black ink.

　◆The Chief Cabinet Secretary は「（1.　　　　　　　[日本語で]）」の意味。
　◆in two characters「2文字で」の in は「（…の方法）で」の意味で，手段を表す。
　◆in black ink「黒インクで」の in は「（…の材料）で」の意味で，素材を表す。
　訳：---

⑦ "Reiwa" comes from characters (**used** in an introduction to some poems in the *Manyoshu*, an ancient anthology of Japanese poetry).

　◆過去分詞の形容詞用法。名詞の後ろに付いて形容詞のようにどのような character かを説明（限定）している。character は「（2.　　　　　　[日本語で]）」の意味。
　◆the *Manyoshu* と an ancient anthology of Japanese poetry は同格の関係。
　訳：---

⑯ People around the world are now waiting to see **whether** Japan will contribute to world peace in this new era.

　◆whether は名詞節を導き，「…かどうか」を意味する。see の目的語となっている。
　訳：---

Part 2 教科書 p.72 ◀意味のまとまりに注意して，本文全体を聞こう。 ◉1-44

①How has the era name in Japan / been determined? // ②What meaning does it have / to Japanese people? //

[1] ③The first imperial era in Japan / dates back to Taika / in 645. // ④The notion of imperial era naming / was established / in 701, / when the Taiho era began. // ⑤The names were quoted / from classical Chinese literature. // ⑥Reiwa, / on the other hand, / was taken / from the *Manyoshu*, / the oldest collection of Japanese poetry. //

[2] ⑦It is said / that the *Manyoshu* was compiled / mainly during the Nara Period, / and it contains / about 4,500 poems. // ⑧The authors ranged / from celebrated poets to nameless farmers. // ⑨Public servants / living alone far away from their families / also contributed. // ⑩When they made poems, / they were able to forget / their everyday work / for a while / and think of their loved ones / at home. //

[3] ⑪The name Reiwa / comes from a line / in an introductory passage / in the *Manyoshu* / which says, / "It is now auspicious early spring; / the weather is fine, / and the wind is soft." // ⑫This line describes a party / for viewing *ume* blossoms / under a sunny spring sky. // ⑬*Ume* blossoms came from China, / and they were new / to the Japanese / at that time. // ⑭They enjoyed *ume* blossoms / and made poems / about them. //

◀意味のまとまりに注意して，本文全体を音読しよう。（199 Words）

Words and Phrases　新出単語・表現の意味を調べよう			
determine 動 [dɪtə́ːrmɪn] B1	1.	date back to …	2.
notion 名 [nóuʃ(ə)n] B1	3.	establish 動 [ɪstǽblɪʃ] A2	4.
quote 動 [kwóut] B2	5.	classical 形 [klǽsɪk(ə)l] B1	6.
literature 名 [lít(ə)rətʃər] B1	7.	compile 動 [kəmpáɪl] B2	8.

author 图[ɔ́:θər] A2	9.	range 動[réɪn(d)ʒ] A2	10.
range from A to B	11.	poet 图[póʊət] B1	12.
nameless 形[néɪmləs]	13.	auspicious 形[ɔ:spíʃəs]	14.

A 【Comprehension 1】 Fill in the blanks in Japanese.

パラグラフごとの要点を整理しよう【思考力・判断力・表現力】

1	元号は中国の（1.　　　　　　）から引用されていたが，「令和」は（2.　　　　　　）から引用された。
2	（2.　　　　　　）は主に（3.　　　　　　）時代に編纂されたもので，さまざまな階級の人々の気持ちが詠まれている。
3	「令和」の名前は（2.　　　　　　）の序文に由来し，春先に（4.　　　　　　）を見て楽しむ様子が描写されている。

B 【Comprehension 2】 Answer the following questions in English.

本文のポイントについて答えよう【思考力・判断力・表現力】

1. When does the first imperial era in Japan date back to?

　--

2. How many poems does the *Manyoshu* contain?

　--

3. What does the name Reiwa come from?

　--

C 【Key Sentences】 Translate the following sentences.

重要文について確認しよう【知識・技能】【思考力・判断力・表現力】

④ The notion of imperial era naming was established in 701, (**when** the Taiho era began).

◆when 以下が関係副詞節となり，西暦701年に補足の情報を追加している。関係副詞の非制限用法である。

訳:--

⑪ The name Reiwa comes from a line in an introductory passage in the *Manyoshu* (which says, ….)

◆関係代名詞 which の節が先行詞 a line (in an introductory passage in the *Manyoshu*) を修飾している。

訳:--

Part 3　教科書 p.74　🔊意味のまとまりに注意して，本文全体を聞こう。　◉1-46

4 ①When we look around the world, / we see different notions of eras. // ②In Western countries, / the birth of Jesus Christ / became the norm / in the Gregorian calendar. // ③In this calendar, / "B.C." means "Before Christ" / and "A.D." means "Anno Domini," / which stands for / "in the year of the Lord" / in Latin. //

5 ④In ancient China, / Emperor Wu started / to name eras / in 114 B.C. // ⑤He changed the era names / when rare natural phenomena appeared / or good things happened. // ⑥For example, / it is said / that he changed the era name / after he saw a comet in the sky / and after he hunted a white kylin, / a legendary animal / in ancient China. //

6 ⑦China was such a large and influential country / that neighboring countries followed the Chinese custom / of naming eras. // ⑧In Japan, / for example, / Emperor Ichijo / changed the era to Eiso / in 989, / due to the close approach of Halley's Comet. // ⑨In 1912, / China abandoned the system of era names / and has never used it since. // ⑩Japan is now the only country / where both the Gregorian calendar and era names are used. //

🔊意味のまとまりに注意して，本文全体を音読しよう。（178 Words）

Words and Phrases	新出単語・表現の意味を調べよう		
Jesus Christ [dʒíːzəs kráist]	イエス（キリスト）	norm 名[nɔ́ːrm]	1.
Gregorian 形[ɡrɪɡɔ́ːriən]	グレゴリオ暦の	Anno Domini 副[ǽnoʊdɑ́(ː)məniː]	2.
stand for …	3.	lord 名[lɔ́ːrd]	4.
emperor 名[émp(ə)rər] B1	5.	Wu [wúː]	武帝
rare 形[réər] B1	6.	phenomena 名 [fənɑ́(ː)mɪnə] B1	phenomenon の複数形
phenomenon 名 [fənɑ́(ː)mənɑ̀(ː)n] B1	7.	comet 名[kɑ́(ː)mɪt] B1	8.
kylin 名[kíːlɪn]	9.	legendary 形 [lédʒ(ə)ndèri] B2	10.

such ... that 〜	11.	influential 形 [ìnfluénʃ(ə)l] B2	12.
Halley [hǽli]	ハリー，ハレー	abandon 動 [əbǽnd(ə)n] B1	13.

A 【Comprehension 1】 Fill in the blanks in Japanese.

パラグラフごとの要点を整理しよう【思考力・判断力・表現力】

4	西洋のグレゴリオ暦ではキリストの誕生を（1.　　　　　）とし「B.C.」と「A.D.」を使う。
5	（2.　　　　　　　　　　）年，中国の皇帝が時代に名を付け始めた。 元号を変えた理由の例：皇帝が珍しい自然現象である（3.　　　　　）を見た。
6	中国の影響で，日本も元号を付けるようになった。 中国が元号制度を中止した今，日本はグレゴリオ暦と元号の両方を使う唯一の国である。

B 【Comprehension 2】 Answer the following questions in English.

本文のポイントについて答えよう【思考力・判断力・表現力】

1. Who started to name eras in ancient China?

---

2. When did China abandon the system of era names?

C 【Key Sentences】 Fill in the blanks and translate the following sentences.

重要文について確認しよう【知識・技能】【思考力・判断力・表現力】

③ In this calendar, "B.C." means "Before Christ" and "A.D." means "Anno Domini," **which** stands for "in the year of the Lord" in Latin.

◆関係代名詞 which の節は先行詞（1.　　　　　[英語2語で]）を詳しく述べている。

訳：

⑥ For example, **it is said that** he changed the era name after he saw a comet in the sky and after he hunted a white **kylin, a legendary animal in ancient China**.

◆it is said that ... は「…と言われている」の意味。〈... is said to 〜〉の形で書きかえることができる。
◆kylin と a legendary animal in ancient China は同格の関係。

訳：

⑩ Japan is now the only country **where** both the Gregorian calendar and era names are used.

◆関係副詞 where の節が先行詞（2.　　　　　[英語3語で]）を修飾している。

訳：

Part 4　教科書 p.76〜p.77　◁意味のまとまりに注意して，本文全体を聞こう。◉1-48

⑦ ①Recent era names in Japan / have signified a common feeling / shared by Japanese people. // ②For example, / they remember Heisei / as a peaceful period. // ③There were no wars in Japan / in the Heisei era. // ④The Heisei Emperor often went / to World War II memorial sites / and prayed that the spirits of the war dead / would rest in peace. // ⑤This gave Japanese people deep comfort. //

⑧ ⑥On the day when the era name Reiwa was announced, / the Prime Minister expressed his hope / that the new era would lead to a bright future. // ⑦He interpreted Reiwa / as a time / when people's beautiful hearts and minds would create a new culture. // ⑧People in Japan / hold wishes for world peace. // ⑨One woman said, / "I hope / that all children can grow strong in peace / in the new era." //

⑨ ⑩More than 200 era names have been used / in Japan, / and each era witnessed / both good and sad events. // ⑪Most of those events / might not be recorded / in history books, / but they surely remain / in our deep memories. // ⑫What memory in the new era / will be handed down / to future generations? //

◁意味のまとまりに注意して，本文全体を音読しよう。（182 Words）

Words and Phrases　新出単語・表現の意味を調べよう			
signify 動 [sígnɪfàɪ] B2	1.	memorial 形 [məmɔ́:riəl]	2.
pray 動 [préɪ] A2	3.	in peace	4.
comfort 名 [kʌ́mfərt] B1	5.	prime 形 [práɪm] B2	6.
minister 名 [mínɪstər] B2	7.	interpret 動 [ɪntə́:ァprət] B2	8.
interpret A as B	9.	witness 動 [wítnəs] B1	10.

A 【Comprehension 1】 Fill in the blanks in Japanese.

パラグラフごとの要点を整理しよう【思考力・判断力・表現力】

7	日本の元号は日本の人々が共有する感情を表してきた。 （例）平成：「(1.　　　　) な時代」 　　平成の天皇は（2.　　　　　　　　　　) の追悼の地を訪れ，戦没者に祈りを捧げた。
8	内閣総理大臣の「令和」の時代に対する希望 　➡新時代が（3.　　　　　　　　　　) へとつながること
9	日本では（4.　　　　　　) 種類以上の元号が使われており，それぞれの時代はよい出来事や（5.　　　　　) 出来事を目撃してきた。 それらの大部分は歴史書に記録されていないかもしれないが，私たちの（6.　　　　　) 記憶の中に残っている。

B 【Comprehension 2】 Answer the following questions in English.

本文のポイントについて答えよう【思考力・判断力・表現力】

1. What did the Heisei Emperor often do?

　　...

2. On the day when the era name Reiwa was announced, what hope did the Prime Minister express?

　　...

3. What events did each era witness?

　　...

C 【Key Sentences】 Translate the following sentences.

重要文について確認しよう【知識・技能】【思考力・判断力・表現力】

⑥ On the day (**when** the era name Reiwa was announced), the Prime Minister expressed his hope **that** the new era **would** lead to a bright future.

◆関係副詞 when の節が the day を説明する。
◆〈名詞＋that-節〉で，「～という…」という意味になり，that-節が前の名詞 his hope を詳しく説明する同格の用法である。
◆would は過去から見た未来を表している。

訳：...

⑦ He interpreted Reiwa as a time (**when** people's beautiful hearts and minds **would** create a new culture).

◆関係副詞 when の節が a time を説明する。
◆would は過去から見た未来を表している。

訳：...

Activity Plus 〔教科書 p.80～p.81〕 🔊意味のまとまりに注意して，本文全体を聞こう。 ◉1-50

①In English class, / your teacher gave a worksheet / to your group. // ②You are listening / to a group discussing / a student's translation / of a *haiku*. //

③Task // ④Translate the *haiku* below / into English. //

⑤Tips // ⑥Translate it / in three lines. // ⑦Start each line / with a small letter. // ⑧You don't need / a period / at the end. // ⑨Use short and simple words. // ⑩Try not to use / "I" or "you." //

⑪Use nouns, / rather than verbs / or adjectives. // ⑫If you use verbs, / use them / in the present tense. // ⑬Don't worry / about grammar / too much. //

⑭Translation //

⑮・When you eat a persimmon, / you can hear / a bell toll / at Horyuji. // (Satoshi) //

Satoshi: ⑯I made my translation / as clear and easy / to comprehend / as possible. // ⑰What do you think of it, / Kazuki? //

Kazuki: ⑱You did a good job, / but I think / this is too long / for a translation / of a *haiku*. // ⑲Also, / we should try not to use / "you." // ⑳Can't we make it simpler / and make it sound / more like *haiku*? //

Emily: ㉑I agree with Kazuki. // ㉒In English *haiku*, / we don't have to start / with a capital letter. // ㉓We should make it / in three lines. // ㉔I think / the first line should be something / like "eat a persimmon." //

Satoshi: ㉕Very good, / Emily! // ㉖Then, / the second line can be / "and a bell will toll." // ㉗The final line can be / "at Horyuji." // ㉘Let's put the lines / together! //

㉙eat a persimmon /

and a bell will toll /

at Horyuji //

🔊意味のまとまりに注意して，本文全体を音読しよう。(230 Words)

Words and Phrases 新出単語・表現の意味を調べよう			
worksheet 名[wɚ́ːrkʃìːt]	1.	translate 動[trǽnsleɪt] B1	2.
translate A into B	3.	tip 名[típ] A2	4.

start A with B	5.	noun 名[náʊn] A2	6.
rather 副[rǽðər] A2	7.	rather than …	8.
verb 名[və́ːrb] A2	9.	adjective 名[ǽdʒɪktɪv] A2	10.
tense 名[téns] B1	11.	persimmon 名 [pəːrsímən]	12.
toll 動[tóʊl]	13.	comprehend 動 [kà(ː)mprɪhénd]	14.

A 【**Comprehension 1**】 Fill in the blanks in Japanese.

要点を整理しよう【思考力・判断力・表現力】

課題 俳句を英語に訳す。
ヒント 3行で訳す。各行は（1.　　　　　　）で始める。文末に（2.　　　　　　）は必要ない。
短く簡単な語を使う。I や you は使わないようにする。動詞や形容詞よりも（3.　　　　　　）
を使う。もし動詞を使う場合は，（4.　　　　　　）形にする。文法を気にしすぎない。
[サトシが英訳した俳句を元に話し合い]

発表者	考え [意見]
カズキ	長すぎるので，（5.　　　　　　）を使わないようにして，よりシンプルにしてはどうか。
エミリー	（6.　　　　　　）で始める必要はなく，3行にする。

B 【**Comprehension 2**】 Answer the following questions in English.

本文のポイントについて答えよう【思考力・判断力・表現力】

1. When we use verbs in translating *haiku*, what tense do we use?

----

2. How did Satoshi make his translation?

C 【**Key Sentences**】 Fill in the blank and translate the following sentences.

重要文について確認しよう【知識・技能】【思考力・判断力・表現力】

⑩ Try **not to** use "I" or "you."
◆to-不定詞の否定形は not to 〜。try not to 〜は「〜（1.　　　　　　[日本語で])」の意味。
訳 :---

⑳ Can't we **make** it simpler and **make** it sound more like *haiku*?
◆最初の make は〈make＋O＋C〉の第5文型を作る動詞，後の make は〈make＋O＋動詞の原形〉
を作る使役動詞。
訳 :---

Part 1 教科書 p.86〜p.87 ◁意味のまとまりに注意して，本文全体を聞こう。 ◎1-52

① You want / to gather information / about food loss and waste. // ② You found / a Q&A site. //

③ Is it true / that there is enough food / to feed all the people / on the earth? //

④ It's true / that we can feed everyone / on the earth. // ⑤ For example, / about 2.6 billion metric tons of cereals / are produced annually / all over the world. // ⑥ If they were distributed evenly / to all of the people / around the world, / each person could have / over 330 kilograms of cereals to eat / in a year. // ⑦ That is more than double the amount / that a Japanese consumes / in a year. //

⑧ Nevertheless, / it is also true / that more than 820 million people, / or one in nine people / in the world, / are suffering / from hunger. // ⑨ This implies / that food is not equally available / to everyone. // ⑩ In fact, / about half the cereals produced worldwide / are consumed / in developed countries, / whose population is less than 20% / of the world population. //

⑪ Moreover, / the truth is / that about one third of the food / produced for human consumption / is lost or wasted / every year. // ⑫ This amounts to / about 1.3 billion metric tons. // ⑬ If we save one fourth of the lost or wasted food, / we will save enough food / for all the hungry people / in the world. //

◁意味のまとまりに注意して，本文全体を音読しよう。（207 Words）

Words and Phrases 新出単語・表現の意味を調べよう			
hunger 名 [hʌ́ŋɡər] B1	1.	metric 形 [métrɪk] B2	2.
cereal 名 [síəriəl] A2	3.	annually 副 [ǽnju(ə)li] B1	4.
distribute 動 [dɪstríbjuːt] B1	5.	distribute A to B	6.
evenly 副 [íːvnli] B1	7.	consume 動 [kənsúːm] B1	8.
nevertheless 副 [nèvərðəlés] B1	9.	imply 動 [ɪmpláɪ] B2	10.
equally 副 [íːkw(ə)li] B1	11.	moreover 副 [mɔːróuvər] B1	12.
truth 名 [trúːθ] A2	13.	amount to …	14.

A 【**Comprehension 1**】 Fill in the blanks in Japanese.

要点を整理しよう【思考力・判断力・表現力】

地球には十分な食料があるのか。
・世界では年間で約26億トンの穀物が生産されている。 ➡️もし平等に分配されたら，年間１人当たり（1.　　　）キロ以上の穀物を消費することになり，地球上の人々は十分な食料を得ることになる。 ➡️しかし，世界の９分の１の人は（2.　　　　　）で苦しんでいる。
・なぜ（2.　　　　　）で苦しんでいる人がいるのか。 ➡️（3.　　　　　）の人口は世界の人口の20％未満なのに，すべての穀物のうち約半分が（3.　　　　　）で消費される。 ➡️毎年，人間の消費用の食料の約（4.　　　　　）がむだになっている。そのうち（5.　　　　　）をなくすと，世界中の人に十分な食料が行き届く。

B 【**Comprehension 2**】 Answer the following questions in English.

本文のポイントについて答えよう【思考力・判断力・表現力】

1. How many people are suffering from hunger?

   ----

2. How much food produced for human consumption is lost or wasted every year?

   ----

3. What should we do to save enough food for all the hungry people in the world?

C 【**Key Sentences**】 Fill in the blank and translate the following sentences.

重要文について確認しよう【知識・技能】【思考力・判断力・表現力】

⑥ **If** they **were distributed** evenly to all of the people around the world, each person **could have** over 330 kilograms of cereals to eat in a year.
   ◆仮定法過去の文で，実際には世界の人々に平等に食料が分配されていないことを示す。
   訳：--

⑨ **This implies that** food is not equally available to everyone.
   ◆ imply that S＋V は「S が V することを意味［示唆］する」の意味。
   ◆ This ＝ (1.　　　　　　　　　　　　　　　　[日本語で]）
   訳：--

⑩ About half the cereals (produced worldwide) are consumed in developed countries, **whose** population is less than 20% of the world population.
   ◆関係代名詞 whose は非制限用法で使うことができる。先行詞は developed countries。
   ◆ produced は過去分詞で，the cereals を修飾している。
   訳：--

Part 2 教科書 p.88〜p.89 ◁意味のまとまりに注意して，本文全体を聞こう。 ◎1-54

① The world population / is estimated to reach 9.7 billion / in 2050, / and global food problems / are expected to become / even more serious. //

1 ② Too much food produced / for human beings / is lost or wasted / in the food supply chain. // ③ Food loss occurs / early in the chain / ── before the food even gets / to stores and consumers. // ④ For example, / in developing countries, / farmers lose / a large part of their crops / because they don't have / appropriate storage equipment. // ⑤ Food is often eaten / by bugs and small creatures. // ⑥ Furthermore, / food is sometimes lost / during transportation. // ⑦ For instance, / food may go bad / if it is transported / in trucks without refrigeration. //

2 ⑧ On the other hand, / food waste occurs / at the end of the chain / ── in stores, / restaurants / and houses. // ⑨ Food that is past its best-before date / is discarded / at grocery stores, / and uneaten food is thrown away / at restaurants. // ⑩ In our home, / leftover food goes bad / in the fridge / and is thrown away. //

3 ⑪ Having recognized the importance / of reducing food loss and waste, / the United Nations is encouraging people / to take action. // ⑫ As one of the targets / of SDGs, / we need to reduce food waste / by half / and cut down the amount / of food loss / by 2030. // ⑬ Governments, / organizations / and individuals around the world / have begun / to make efforts / to achieve this target. //

◁意味のまとまりに注意して，本文全体を音読しよう。（218 Words）

Words and Phrases	新出単語・表現の意味を調べよう		
get to …	1.	crop 名 [krá(:)p] B1	2.
appropriate 形 [əpróupriət] A2	3.	storage 名 [stɔ́:rɪdʒ] B1	4.
equipment 名 [ɪkwípmənt] B1	5.	bug 名 [bʌ́g] A2	6.
creature 名 [krí:tʃər] A2	7.	furthermore 副 [fə́:rðərmɔ̀:r] B1	8.
go bad	9.	transport 動 [trænspɔ́:rt] B2	10.
refrigeration 名 [rɪfrɪ̀dʒəréɪʃ(ə)n]	11.	at the end of …	12.
discard 動 [dɪská:rd]	13.	grocery 名 [gróʊs(ə)ri]	14.
uneaten 形 [ʌní:t(ə)n]	15.	leftover 形 [léftòʊvər]	16.

cut down …	17.	individual 名 [ìndɪvídʒu(ə)l] B2	18.

A 【Comprehension 1】 Fill in the blanks in Japanese.

パラグラフごとの要点を整理しよう【思考力・判断力・表現力】

日本のフードロス・フードウェイスト

・食料供給の
（1.　　　　　）に
起こる。
・たとえば発展途上国で適
切な（2.　　　　　）が
なかったり，昆虫や小さ
な生き物に食べられたり，
輸送するときに腐ったり
する。

・食料供給の（3.　　　　　）
に起こる。
・たとえばレストランやお店や
家庭では，期限切れの食料や
残ったものを（4.　　　　　）
してしまう。

国連は SDGs の目標の１つに
フードロス・フードウェイスト
の削減を入れた。

B 【Comprehension 2】 Answer the following questions in English.

本文のポイントについて答えよう【思考力・判断力・表現力】

1. Which occurs early in the food supply chain, food loss or food waste?

2. According to one of the SDG targets, by what year do we need to halve food waste?

C 【Key Sentences】 Fill in the blanks and translate the following sentences.

重要文について確認しよう【知識・技能】【思考力・判断力・表現力】

⑧ **On the other hand**, food waste occurs at **the end of the chain** —— in stores, restaurants and houses.

◆ on the other hand は「一方」の意味で，前に述べられたことと対照的なことを述べるディスコースマーカー。
◆ダッシュは the end of the chain の具体的な内容を同格的に追加している。
◆ the chain＝the （1.　　　　[英語2語で]） chain
訳 :

⑪ **Having recognized** the importance of reducing food loss and waste, the United Nations is **encouraging** people **to** take action.

◆完了形の分詞構文 Having recognized は，分詞構文が表す「時」が主節動詞の表す「時」よりも以前であることを明確にする。主節動詞はここでは is encouraging。
◆ encourage＋O＋to ～は「O に～するよう（2.　　　　　[日本語で]）」の意味。
訳 :

Part 3 教科書 p.90 🔊意味のまとまりに注意して，本文全体を聞こう。 💿1-56

4️⃣ ①France was the first country / to make a law / to reduce food waste. // ②Since 2016, / large supermarkets have been prohibited / from throwing away food. // ③Instead, / they have been required / to donate it / or turn it into compost / or animal feed. // ④France has become a leader / in food waste reduction / and has inspired / other countries. //

5️⃣ ⑤In the Spanish town of Galdakao, / a community refrigerator was placed / on a sidewalk / in 2015. // ⑥People from nearby restaurants and households / put their excess food and leftovers / into the fridge, / and whoever wants them / can take them / for free. // ⑦The movement of setting up community refrigerators / has been spreading / to many other countries, / including the U.K., / Belgium, / Argentina / and Israel. //

6️⃣ ⑧October 16 is "World Food Day," / which was established / by the United Nations. // ⑨In Japan, / the entire month of October / has been designated / as "World Food Day Month." // ⑩During this period, / various food events are held / all over Japan. // ⑪For example, / in an event / in 2019, / participants were asked / to post recipes / using unused food / on social media. // ⑫Sponsors of the event / donated 120 yen / per post to a charity / that supported school meals / in Africa. //

🔊意味のまとまりに注意して，本文全体を音読しよう。(191 Words)

Words and Phrases 新出単語・表現の意味を調べよう			
prohibit 動[prouhíbət] B2	1.	prohibit A from B	2.
require 動[rɪkwáɪər] B1	3.	require … to 〜	4.
compost 名[ká(:)mpoust]	5.	reduction 名 [rɪdʌ́kʃ(ə)n] B1	6.
Galdakao [gà(:)ldəká(:)ou]	ガルダカオ	refrigerator 名 [rɪfrídʒərèɪtər] A2	7.
sidewalk 名[sáɪdwɔ̀:k] B1	8.	nearby 形[nìərbáɪ] B1	9.
household 名 [háʊshòʊld] B1	10.	excess 形[ɪksés]	11.
whoever 代[huévər] B1	12.	for free	13.
Belgium 名[béldʒəm]	14.	Argentina 名 [à:rdʒ(ə)ntí:nə]	15.

Israel 名[ízriəl]	16.	designate 動[dézɪgnèɪt]	17.
designate A as B	18.	unused 形[ʌnjúːzd]	19.

A 【**Comprehension 1**】 Fill in the blanks in Japanese.

パラグラフごとの要点を整理しよう【思考力・判断力・表現力】

フードウェイストを削減するための取り組み

フランス
　2016年以降，大型スーパーは，食料を捨てることが禁止され，代わりに
(1.　　　　　) する，もしくは肥料や飼料にすることが要求されている。

日本
　2019年のイベントで，主催者はアフリカの
(4.　　　　　) を支えるための慈善団体に寄付をした。

(2.　　　　　)・イギリス・ベルギー・アルゼンチン・イスラエル
　残った食料を公共の (3.　　　　　) に入れ，それをだれもが無料で利用できるようにした。

B 【**Comprehension 2**】 Answer the following questions in English.

本文のポイントについて答えよう【思考力・判断力・表現力】

1. Which country is a leader in food waste reduction?

　　...

2. How can people use a community refrigerator?

　　...

3. What is the date of "World Food Day"?

　　...

C 【**Key Sentences**】 Fill in the blanks and translate the following sentences.

重要文について確認しよう【知識・技能】【思考力・判断力・表現力】

③ **Instead**, **they** have been required to donate **it** or turn **it** into compost or animal feed.

　◆instead「その代わりに，そうではなく」。ここでは「(1.　　　　　[日本語で]) のではなく」の意味。

　◆they は (2.　　　　　[英語2語で])，2つの it は (3.　　　　　[英語で]) を指す。

　訳：...

⑥ **Whoever** wants **them** can take **them** for free.
　　　　　ˢ

　◆複合関係詞 whoever は「…する人はだれでも」の意味。単数扱い。

　◆2つの them はいずれも (4.　　　　　[英語4語で]) を指す。

　訳：...

59

Part 4 教科書 p.92 ◀意味のまとまりに注意して，本文全体を聞こう。 ◎1-58

[7] ①Another way / to tackle the problem of food loss and waste / is to use technology. // ②Recently, / various food-sharing apps have been developed / and are receiving special attention. // ③These apps help match people / who don't want to discard food / with people who need it. //

[8] ④Some apps connect a person / to another person. // ⑤When you have more food / than you can eat / in your home, / you can use these apps / to find someone / to share it with. // ⑥Other apps link retailers / to shoppers. // ⑦A supermarket can post discount information / about unsold food. // ⑧Shoppers can purchase / this unsold food cheaply / with the app / and come to the supermarket later / to pick it up. // ⑨There are also some apps / that connect stores / to charity organizations. // ⑩When a restaurant has a surplus of food / that will spoil soon, / it can donate the food. // ⑪These apps help reduce / food loss and waste / at every point / along the food supply chain. //

[9] ⑫Food loss and waste / is a global issue. // ⑬Everyone in the world / has to understand / the causes of this problem / and make an effort / to solve it. // ⑭When these efforts bear fruit, / we will finally have a world / free of hunger. //

◀意味のまとまりに注意して，本文全体を音読しよう。（195 Words）

Words and Phrases 新出単語・表現の意味を調べよう			
tackle 動[tǽk(ə)l] B2	1.	match A with B	2.
retailer 名[ríːtèɪlər] B2	3.	shopper 名[ʃá(ː)pər] B1	4.
discount 名[dískaʊnt] B1	5.	unsold 形[ʌnsóʊld]	6.
purchase 動[pə́ːrtʃəs] B2	7.	surplus 名[sə́ːrpləs]	8.
spoil 動[spɔ́ɪl] A2	9.	bear fruit	10.
free of ...	11.		

A 【Comprehension 1】 Fill in the blanks in Japanese.

パラグラフごとの要点を整理しよう【思考力・判断力・表現力】

フードロス・フードウェイストの問題に対処するアプリ		
人と人をつなぐ	小売店と買い物客をつなぐ	店と（3.　　　　　）をつなぐ
自宅で残りそうな食べ物を（1.　　　　　）ことができる人を探すことができる。	スーパーで売れ残った食べ物を，アプリを使って（2.　　　　　）で購入し，後で店に取りに行く。	店で残ったものを（4.　　　　　）できる。

B 【Comprehension 2】 Answer the following questions in English.

本文のポイントについて答えよう【思考力・判断力・表現力】

1. What kind of technology has been developed to solve the food problem?

2. What can supermarkets do to help reduce food waste?

3. In order to have a world free of hunger, what should we do?

C 【Key Sentences】 Fill in the blanks and translate the following sentences.

重要文について確認しよう【知識・技能】【思考力・判断力・表現力】

① **Another** way to tackle the problem of food loss and waste is to use technology.
　　　　　　　　　　　S　　　　　　　　　　　　　　　　　　　V　　C
　◆ another は「もう1つの」。解決策を「法整備」「（1.　　　　　　[日本語で]）」「世界食料デイ」のほかにもう1つ提示している。
　訳：

③ These apps **help match** |people (who don't want to discard food)| with |people (who need **it**)|.
　◆ help (to) ＋動詞の原形「～する手助けをする」。
　◆ match A with B の A と B はいずれも，people が関係代名詞 who で修飾された句。
　　it ＝ (2.　　　　　[英語で])。
　訳：

⑭ When these efforts bear fruit, we will finally have a world (free of hunger).
　◆形容詞 free が前置詞句をともない，a world を後置修飾している。
　訳：

Activity Plus 教科書 p.96～p.97 ◁意味のまとまりに注意して，本文全体を聞こう。 ◎1-60

①You responded / to an online questionnaire / made by your Assistant Language Teacher. // ②After all the students answered, / a slide with a graph was generated. //

Introduction //

③I am studying / about food loss and waste / in daily life. // ④I would like to ask you / to fill out this questionnaire. // ⑤It only takes / about five minutes. // ⑥The results will be used / for my study, / and I will give a research presentation / at a later date. // ⑦Thank you / in advance / for your help. //

⑧Questionnaire / about food loss and waste //

⑨Are you or your family members doing something / to reduce food waste / in your home? // ⑩Please check all the actions / that are true for your family, / and then check who is/are doing them. // ⑪You may choose / more than one option. //

◁意味のまとまりに注意して，本文全体を音読しよう。（125 Words）

Words and Phrases 新出単語・表現の意味を調べよう			
questionnaire 名 [kwèstʃənéər] B1	1.	respond 動 [rɪspá(:)nd] B1	2.
respond to …	3.	online 形 [à(:)nláɪn] A2	4.
assistant 形 [əsíst(ə)nt] A2	5.	slide 名 [sláɪd] A2	6.
advance 名 [ədvǽns] B2	7.	in advance	8.
option 名 [á(:)pʃ(ə)n] B1	9.	make A from B	10.
pickle 名 [pík(ə)l] B2	11.		

A 【Comprehension 1】 Fill in the blanks in Japanese.

要点を整理しよう【思考力・判断力・表現力】

> アンケートにかかる時間：約（1.　　　　）分
> アンケートのテーマ：フードロスとフードウェイスト
>
> 質問内容：あなたやあなたの家族は，家でフードウェイストを（2.　　　　　　）ために何かし
> 　　　　　ていますか。
> 1．スーパーマーケットに行く前に買い物リストを作成する。
> 2．毎回余分なものを買わないよう，何度もスーパーマーケットに行く。
> 3．（3.　　　　　　　　　）を気にしすぎない。
> 4．残り物を捨てずに，（4.　　　　　　）に保存する。
> 5．家族が食べきれない量を調理しない。
> 6．使わなかった野菜を（5.　　　　　　）にする

B 【Comprehension 2】 Answer the following questions in English.

本文のポイントについて答えよう【思考力・判断力・表現力】

1. Why did the ALT make the online questionnaire?

　--

2. According to the graph, who is the most active in reducing household food waste?

　--

3. According to the graph, who tends to make pickles from unused vegetables?

　--

C 【Key Sentences】 Fill in the blank and translate the following sentences.

重要文について確認しよう【知識・技能】【思考力・判断力・表現力】

① You responded to an online questionnaire (**made** by your Assistant Language Teacher).

　◆ made は過去分詞で，an online questionnaire を修飾する。

　訳：--

⑨ Are you or your family members doing something **to reduce** food waste in your home?

　◆ to reduce は to-不定詞の副詞用法で，目的を表す。

　訳：--

⑩ Check who **is/are** doing **them**.

　◆ is/are は，is or are と読む。
　◆ them＝the（1.　　　　　　[英語で]）

　訳：--

Part 1 教科書 p.102〜p.103 🔊意味のまとまりに注意して，本文全体を聞こう。 ◎2-2

①Koji and an Assistant Language Teacher are talking / about a map / of the world. //

Koji: ②What's that? //

ALT: ③Hi, / Koji! // ④It's a map / that shows the highest mountain / on each continent. //

Koji: ⑤Wow, / how interesting! // ⑥I know / you like climbing mountains. // ⑦Where would you like to go? //

ALT: ⑧I want / to climb Mt. Everest / someday. // ⑨Do you know / about the Explorer's Grand Slam? // ⑩It is the accomplishment / of climbing the highest mountain / on each continent, / including Mt. Everest, / and going to the North and South Poles. //

Koji: ⑪Oh, / wow! // ⑫That must be / very hard / to do. // ⑬How many people / have done it? //

ALT: ⑭About 50 people / have done it / so far! // ⑮And a female Japanese university student / became the youngest person / in the world / to complete this great achievement / in 2017. //

🔊意味のまとまりに注意して，本文全体を音読しよう。（125 Words）

Words and Phrases 新出単語・表現の意味を調べよう			
dialogue 名[dáɪələːɡ] B1	1.	Denali [dənáːli]	デナリ山
Alaska [əlǽskə]	アラスカ州	Elbrus [ɪlbrúːs]	エルブルース山
Everest [év(ə)rɪst]	エベレスト山	Tibet [tɪbét]	チベット
Nepal 名[nəpɔ́ːl]	2.	Aconcagua [àːkɔːŋkáːgwɑ]	アコンカグア山
Vinson Massif [víns(ə)n mæsíːf]	ヴィンソン山 [ヴィンソン・マシフ]	Kilimanjaro [kìlɪməndʒáːrou]	キリマンジャロ山
Tanzania 名[tænzəníːə]	3.	Kosciuszko [kàzɪáskou]	コジアスコ山
Antarctica 名[æntáːrktɪkə]	4.	continent 名 [ká(ː)nt(ə)nənt] A2	5.

explorer 图[ɪksplɔ́ːrər] B2	6.	grand slam 图 [grǽnd slǽm]	7.
accomplishment 图 [əkɑ́(ː)mplɪʃmənt]	8.	pole 图[póʊl] B1	9.
so far	10.		

A 【Comprehension 1】 Fill in the blanks in Japanese.

要点を整理しよう【思考力・判断力・表現力】

探検家グランドスラムとは

・A （1.　　　　　　　） など，
それぞれの （2.　　　　　） にある最高峰に
登頂して，さらに B （3.　　　　　） と
C （4.　　　　　） に到達する挑戦。
・これまでに約 （5.　　） 人が達成した。
➡世界最年少の達成者は日本人女性の大学生で，
（6.　　） 年に達成した。

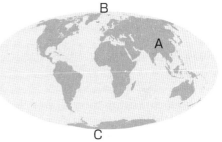

B 【Comprehension 2】 Answer the following questions in English.

本文のポイントについて答えよう【思考力・判断力・表現力】

1. What does the map show?

　..

2. Which mountain does the Assistant Language Teacher want to climb?

　..

3. What have the 50 people they are talking about done?

　..

C 【Key Sentences】 Fill in the blank and translate the following sentences.

重要文について確認しよう【知識・技能】【思考力・判断力・表現力】

⑩ **It** is the accomplishment (of climbing the highest mountain on each continent), **including** Mt. Everest, and going to the North and South Poles.

　◆ including は，動詞 include からできた前置詞で，「…を含めて」 という意味。
　◆ it＝the （1.　　　　　　　　　　　　　[英語3語で]）
　訳：..

⑮ A female Japanese university student became <u>the youngest person in the world</u> (**to complete** this great achievement) in 2017.

　◆ to-不定詞 to complete 以下が，直前の名詞句 the youngest person (in the world) を修飾する。
　訳：..

Part 2 教科書 p.106〜p.107 📢意味のまとまりに注意して，本文全体を聞こう。 🎧2-4

①Marin Minamiya completed a remarkable achievement. // ②What motivated her? // ③What made her reach / for her dream? //

① ④"Strive toward your goal / with passion. // ⑤Nothing is stronger / than our will. // ⑥A person's potential is / truly infinite," / says Marin Minamiya. // ⑦She completed the Explorer's Grand Slam / when she was 20 years old. //

② ⑧Marin was born / in Tokyo / on December 20, / 1996. // ⑨Since her father worked / for a trading company, / her family moved / to various places, / including Malaysia, / mainland China / and Hong Kong. // ⑩She lived / outside Japan / from a young age, / and it was difficult / for her / to identify herself / as Japanese. // ⑪When she was 13 years old / in Hong Kong, / she got an opportunity / to climb some mountains / with her classmates. // ⑫This became a turning point / in her life. // ⑬Each climb taught her / something new, / and afterward / she felt as if she had escaped / from all stress and anxiety. //

③ ⑭One day, / Marin went trekking / in Nepal, / and she saw Mt. Everest / for the first time. // ⑮Everything about the magnificent mountain was / eye-opening for her. // ⑯The experience inspired her / greatly / and provided her / with courage, / faith / and power. // ⑰She said, / "I knew / that I would come back / to the great Everest / one day. // ⑱I wanted / to explore myself / and learn the purpose / of my existence." //

📢意味のまとまりに注意して，本文全体を音読しよう。(211 Words)

Words and Phrases 新出単語・表現の意味を調べよう			
motivate 動[móʊtəvèɪt] B1	1.	reach for …	2.
strive 動[stráɪv] B2	3.	strive toward …	4.
infinite 形[ínfɪnət]	5.	work for …	6.
trading 名[tréɪdɪŋ]	7.	Malaysia 名[məléɪʒə]	8.
mainland 形[méɪnlənd]	9.	Hong Kong [há(:)ŋkà(:)ŋ]	香港
identify 動[aɪdéntəfàɪ] B2	10.	identify A as B	11.
opportunity 名 [à(:)pərtjú:nəti] A2	12.	afterward 副 [ǽftərwərd] B1	13.

anxiety 名 [æŋzáɪəti] B1	14.	trekking 名 [trékɪŋ]	15.
magnificent 形 [mægnífɪs(ə)nt] B1	16.	provide A with B	17.
faith 名 [féɪθ] B2	18.	explore 動 [ɪksplɔ́ːr] A2	19.
existence 名 [ɪgzíst(ə)ns] B1	20.		

A 【Comprehension 1】 Fill in the blanks in Japanese.

パラグラフごとの要点を整理しよう【思考力・判断力・表現力】

1	南谷真鈴さんの言葉 「(1.　　　　) をもって目標に向かって努力してほしい。私たちの (2.　　　　) よりも強いものはない。人の可能性は本当に (3.　　　　) だ。」
2	登山への目覚め ・父親が (4.　　　　) に勤めていた関係で，幼いころから世界中で暮らす。 ・13歳のときに (5.　　　　) でクラスメートといっしょに登山をする機会を持つ。 ➡登山で新しいことを知り，ストレスや (6.　　　　) から逃れるように感じる。
3	エベレストとの出会い ・(7.　　　　) でエベレストの壮大な姿を初めて見て大いに奮起する。 ➡再びエベレストに戻ることを決意する。

B 【Comprehension 2】 Answer the following questions in English.

本文のポイントについて答えよう【思考力・判断力・表現力】

1. What did Marin do when she was 20 years old?

----

2. Who was with Marin when she climbed some mountains in Hong Kong?

C 【Key Sentences】 Fill in the blank and translate the following sentences.

重要文について確認しよう【知識・技能】【思考力・判断力・表現力】

⑬ Each climb taught her something new, and afterward she felt **as if** she had escaped from all stress and anxiety.

◆ as if ... は仮定法とともに用いることができる。仮定法過去完了で「まるで…であったかのように」。

訳: --

⑯ **The experience** inspired her greatly and provided her with courage.

◆ the experience は，初めて見た (1.　　　　 [日本語で]) のすべてが目を見張るように感じられた経験。

訳: --

Part 3 教科書 p.108〜p.109 ◁意味のまとまりに注意して，本文全体を聞こう。 ◉2-6

④ ①When Marin was 17, / she started / preparing for climbing Mt. Everest. // ②She told her father / about her ambition. // ③However, / he said, / "I won't support you / financially. // ④This is your project / and you're old enough / to figure out / what to do / on your own." // ⑤Since she had no assistance, / she had to request support / from companies / while studying and training. // ⑥Some people told her / she would not succeed. // ⑦However, / a strong will arose in her / and defeated such negative words. // ⑧She thought, / "If I give up, / I will be a person / who never tried anything." // ⑨Luckily, / she received financial support / from many firms. //

⑤ ⑩As a first step, / Marin climbed Mt. Aconcagua / in her last year of high school. // ⑪In the following year, / she climbed Mt. Kilimanjaro, / Mont Blanc / and Mt. Manaslu. // ⑫Finally, / the day came / when her dream was realized. // ⑬In May 2016, / at the age of 19, / she was standing on Everest / above the clouds, / above all her difficulties. //

⑥ ⑭Marin's dream kept growing / as she conquered more mountains. // ⑮Never did she stop / challenging herself, / even though some people said / her challenges were impossible. // ⑯She set her sights / on the Seven Summits / and, eventually, / on the Explorer's Grand Slam. //

◁意味のまとまりに注意して，本文全体を音読しよう。（198 Words）

Words and Phrases	新出単語・表現の意味を調べよう			
ambition 名[æmbíʃ(ə)n] A2	1.	financially 副 [fənǽnʃ(ə)li] B2	2.	
figure out …	3.	on one's own	4.	
assistance 名 [əsíst(ə)ns] B1	5.	request 動 [rɪkwést] B1	6.	
succeed 動 [səksíːd] A2	7.	arose 動 [əróuz]	arise の過去形	
arise 動 [əráɪz] B1	8.	negative 形 [négətɪv] A2	9.	
give up	10.	financial 形 [fənǽnʃ(ə)l] B1	11.	
firm 名 [fɚm] B1	12.	Mont Blanc [mɔ̀ːnblɑ́ːŋ]	モンブラン	

Manaslu [mənǽslu:]	マナスル山	conquer 動 [kɑ́(:)ŋkər] B1	13.
set one's sights on …	14.		

A 【**Comprehension 1**】 Fill in the blanks in Japanese.

パラグラフごとの要点を整理しよう【思考力・判断力・表現力】

4	エベレスト登頂に向けての準備 ・17歳のときに準備を始めたが，（1.　　　　　　　）からの経済的援助は得られない。 ➡勉強や研修をしながら（2.　　　　　　　）からの支援を求める。 ➡周囲の（3.　　　　　　）的な言葉を打ち破りながら続けて，多くの支援を受ける。
5	エベレスト登頂の成功 ・（4.　　　　　　）の最終学年でアコンカグアに登り，翌年にキリマンジャロ，モンブラン，マナスルに登る。 ・2016年5月，（5.　　　　　）歳のときにエベレスト登頂に成功する。
6	エベレスト登頂後の新たな目標 ・狙いを七大陸最高峰に定め，最終的に（6.　　　　　　　　　　　　）を目標とする。

B 【**Comprehension 2**】 Answer the following questions in English.

本文のポイントについて答えよう【思考力・判断力・表現力】

1. Why did Marin have to request support for climbing Mt. Everest?

2. Which mountain did Marin start with to prepare for climbing Mt. Everest?

C 【**Key Sentences**】 Fill in the blank and translate the following sentences.

重要文について確認しよう【知識・技能】【思考力・判断力・表現力】

④ **This** is your project and you're old enough to figure out what to do on your own.
　◆ This＝(1.　　　　　　　　　　[日本語で]）
　訳：

⑫ Finally, the day came (**when** her dream was realized).
　◆関係副詞 when を含む節が，先行詞 the day を修飾する。先行詞と関係詞が離れる場合がある。
　訳：

⑮ **Never did she stop** challenging herself, **even though** some people said her challenges were impossible.
　◆否定語 never が強調のために文頭に出て，後ろが疑問文と同じ語順になっている。
　訳：

Part 4 教科書 p.110～p.111 ◁意味のまとまりに注意して，本文全体を聞こう。◎2-8

7 ①Marin has accomplished the Explorer's Grand Slam, / proving that there is nothing / we cannot do / if we keep trying. // ②"Am I what I want to be?" // ③This question made her set out / for the mountains. // ④Climbing mountains / and keeping her motivation / enabled her / to prove herself / and conquer her weaknesses. // ⑤They taught her / that anything could be attained; / any summit could be reached, / no matter how high / it might be. //

8 ⑥Marin is now preparing / for her next adventure. // ⑦She hopes to sail / to various countries / with a human-powered yacht / and talk about life and the future / with children there. // ⑧Marin says, / "To live is to weave your tapestry / with different patterns. // ⑨The patterns and colors in our tapestries / are determined / by how we live. // ⑩We need / to ask ourselves / what we want to do / in order to make / our own special tapestries." //

9 ⑪This is Marin's message / to us all: / "Even though your steps may seem small, / they will surely combine / to become a great leap / to make your future / better. // ⑫Believe that you are going to make it / through everything / you are doing. // ⑬There is nothing / as strong as your passions / to make your dreams come true." // ◁意味のまとまりに注意して，本文全体を音読しよう。(197 Words)

Words and Phrases 新出単語・表現の意味を調べよう			
accomplish 動 [əkά(:)mplɪʃ] B1	1.	prove 動 [prúːv] B1	2.
set out for …	3.	enable 動 [ɪnéɪb(ə)l] B1	4.
enable … to ～	5.	attain 動 [ətéɪn] B1	6.
sail 動 [séɪl] B2	7.	human-powered 形 [hjúːmənpàʊərd]	8.
weave 動 [wíːv]	9.	tapestry 名 [tǽpɪstri]	10.
pattern 名 [pǽtərn] B1	11.	leap 名 [líːp] B2	12.
come true	13.		

A 【Comprehension 1】 Fill in the blanks in Japanese.

パラグラフごとの要点を整理しよう【思考力・判断力・表現力】

7	山々の登頂の挑戦からの気づき ・探検家グランドスラムを達成する。 ➡山に登って（1.　　　　　　　　　　　　）を維持することで弱点を克服する。 ➡どんなことでも成し遂げられるということを山から学ぶ。
8	真鈴さんの次なる目標 ・（2.　　　　　　）で動くヨットでさまざまな国に航海をして，そこにいる子供と話すこと。 ➡「生きることはさまざまな模様のある（3.　　　　　　　　　　）を編むこと。」
9	真鈴さんのメッセージ 「小さく見える歩みでも，結び付いて将来をよくするための大きな（4.　　　　）になる。 夢をかなえるには（5.　　　　　）ほど強いものはない。」

B 【Comprehension 2】 Answer the following questions in English.

本文のポイントについて答えよう【思考力・判断力・表現力】

1. What is the question that made Marin set out for the mountains?

    ----

2. What does Marin want to talk about with children in various countries?

C 【Key Sentences】 Fill in the blanks and translate the following sentences.

重要文について確認しよう【知識・技能】【思考力・判断力・表現力】

④ Climbing mountains and keeping her motivation **enabled** her **to** prove herself and conquer her weaknesses.

◆無生物主語の場合，〈S enable＋O＋to ～〉は「S によって O は～できる」とすると自然な訳になる。

訳：---

⑤ **They** taught her that anything could be attained; any summit could be reached, **no matter how** high **it** might be.

◆ they＝（1.　　　　　　　　　　　　　　　　[英語6語で]），
　 it＝any（2.　　　　　　　　　[英語で]）
◆ no matter は疑問詞などと用いて，「…であろうとも」。no matter how ... の後の語順に注意。

訳：---

⑪ **Even though** your steps may seem small, they will surely combine **to become** a great leap to make your future better.

◆ even though は，ここでは「たとえ…であっても」という意味。
◆ to become は，「結果」を表す to-不定詞と考え，「（その結果）～になる」とすると自然な解釈になる。

訳：---

Activity Plus　教科書 p.116〜p.117　🔊意味のまとまりに注意して，本文全体を聞こう。◎2-10

①In class, / students are sharing / their plans / for the future / while showing charts / about their goals. // ②You are listening / to a student's presentation / about her goals / and action plans. //

③Hi! // Here are my future goals / and the detailed actions / I will take / to achieve them. // ④During high school, / I will improve my academic abilities. // ⑤I study hard / in every class / and at home. // ⑥I'm in the tennis club / and our team has a goal / of participating in the regional tournament. // ⑦All the members of my club / practice very hard. // ⑧During college, / I will broaden my perspectives / and meet many new people / from around the world. // ⑨By the time I'm 30 years old, / I definitely want / to work for a trading company. // ⑩To realize my dream, / I plan to study economics / and gain a good command / of several languages. // ⑪Thank you / for listening. //

🔊意味のまとまりに注意して，本文全体を音読しよう。（142 Words）

Words and Phrases	新出単語・表現の意味を調べよう		
chart 名[tʃáːrt] A2	1.	term 名[táːrm] B1	2.
detailed 形[díːteɪld] B2	3.	regional 形 [ríːdʒ(ə)n(ə)l] B1	4.
broaden 動[brɔ́ːd(ə)n] B2	5.	perspective 名 [pərspéktɪv] B2	6.
academic 形 [ækədémɪk] B1	7.	participate 動 [paːrtísɪpèɪt] B1	8.
participate in ...	9.	by the time ...	10.
definitely 副 [déf(ə)nətli] B1	11.	command 名 [kəmænd] B1	12.

A 【**Comprehension 1**】 Fill in the blanks in Japanese.

要点を整理しよう【思考力・判断力・表現力】

将来の目標と行動計画

> ○高校生の間
> 目標は（1.　　　　）を向上させることとテニスの（2.　　　　）大会に出場すること。そのために，一生懸命に勉強とテニスの練習をしている。

→

> ○大学生の間
> 目標は視野を（3.　　　　）こと。そのために，（4.　　　　）で勉強したり（5.　　　　）活動をしたり，（6.　　　　）の行事に参加しようとしている。

→

> ○30歳になるまで
> 目標は（7.　　　　）で勤務すること。そのために，（8.　　　　）を学び，いくつかの言語を上手に（9.　　　　）できる能力を獲得しようとしている。

B 【**Comprehension 2**】 Answer the following questions in English.

本文のポイントについて答えよう【思考力・判断力・表現力】

1. What does the student do in order to improve her academic abilities?

----

2. What does the student want to do in order to broaden her perspective?

----

3. According to the chart, what will the student do to gain a good command of languages?

C 【**Key Sentences**】 Fill in the blank and translate the following sentences.

重要文について確認しよう【知識・技能】【思考力・判断力・表現力】

① In class, students are sharing their plans for the future **while showing** charts about their goals.

◆ while は接続詞だが，節中の主語と be-動詞が省略されることがある。

訳：---

③ Here are my future goals and <u>the detailed actions</u> (I will take to achieve **them**).

◆ the detailed actions が直後の節で修飾されている。関係代名詞 that が省略されている。

◆ them＝(1.　　　　　　　　　　　　　　[英語3語で])

訳：---

⑨ **By the time** I'm 30 years old, I definitely want to work for a trading company.

◆ by the time … 「…までに」。接続詞のように用いる。節内の動詞は未来のことでも現在形となる。

訳：---

Part 1 教科書 p.122〜p.123 ◀意味のまとまりに注意して，本文全体を聞こう。 ◉2-12

①You have bought a brand-new smartwatch. // ②You are reading / the user manual / to find out / how to charge the watch. //

③STEP 1 //

④Connect the USB plug / of the battery charger / to the port of an AC adapter. //

⑤STEP 2 //

⑥Place the watch / on the charger. // ⑦Make sure / that it touches the charging pins. // ⑧If the watch is correctly connected, / the charging icon will appear / on the watch screen. // ⑨If you cannot see the icon, / you will need / to check the contact / between the charger and the watch. //

⑩STEP 3 //

⑪When the watch fully charges, / "100%" will be displayed / on the watch screen / and the watch will automatically stop charging. // ⑫It takes about one hour / for the watch to charge / fully. //

⑬Notes: //

⑭The proper temperature range for charging is / between 10℃ and 30℃. // ⑮The watch may not charge properly / below or above these temperatures. //

⑯The charger has been developed / specifically for this product. // ⑰The use of an unauthorized charger / may damage the watch. //

⑱Do not try / to change the battery / in the watch. // ⑲The battery is built-in / and should be replaced / only at an authorized service center. //

◀意味のまとまりに注意して，本文全体を音読しよう。（186 Words）

Words 新出単語の意味を調べよう			
manual 名 [mǽnju(ə)l] B2	1.	brand-new 形 [bræn(d)njúː] B1	2.
smartwatch 名 [smáːrtwà(ː)tʃ]	3.	charge 動 [tʃáːrdʒ] B1	4.
plug 名 [plʌ́g] B1	5.	port 名 [pɔ́ːrt] B1	6.
adapter 名 [ədǽptər]	7.	pin 名 [pín] B2	8.

correctly 副[kəréktli] A2	9.	icon 名[áɪkɑ(:)n] B2	10.
display 動[dɪspléɪ] B1	11.	specifically 副 [spəsífɪk(ə)li] B2	12.
unauthorized 形 [ʌnɔ́:θəràɪzd] B2	13.	authorized 形[ɔ́:θəràɪzd]	14.

A 【Comprehension 1】 Fill in the blanks in Japanese.

要点を整理しよう【思考力・判断力・表現力】

STEP 1	充電器の USB プラグを AC アダプタの USB ポートに接続します。
STEP 2	充電器の上にスマートウォッチを置きます。(₁.　　　　　) に確実に接触するようにします。
STEP 3	時計がフル充電になると，画面に100％と表示され，(₂.　　　　　) で充電は停止します。フル充電には (₃.　　) 時間程度かかります。
注意	・充電に適した気温は (₄.　　　　　) で，この温度を下回る，もしくは上回ると正しく充電できないことがあります。 ・認可されていない充電器の使用はスマートウォッチを破損する可能性があります。 ・時計内の (₅.　　　　　) は認定されたサービスセンターで実施してください。

B 【Comprehension 2】 Answer the following questions in English.

本文のポイントについて答えよう【思考力・判断力・表現力】

1. What do you have to do first to charge a smartwatch?

----

2. What happens to the watch when it is correctly connected to the battery charger?

----

3. What may happen if you use an unauthorized charger?

C 【Key Sentences】 Fill in the blank and translate the following sentences.

重要文について確認しよう【知識・技能】【思考力・判断力・表現力】

⑫ **It takes** about one hour for the watch **to** charge fully.

◆〈it takes＋時間＋to-不定詞〉で「～するのに…（時間）がかかる」。

意味上の主語は (₁.　　　　　[英語 2 語で])。

訳:---

$$S \qquad\qquad V \qquad\qquad O$$

⑰ The use of an unauthorized charger　may damage　the watch.

◆名詞句 The use of an unauthorized charger が主語になっている。名詞 use は [júːs] と発音する。

訳:---

Part 2 教科書 p.124〜p.125 ◁意味のまとまりに注意して，本文全体を聞こう。 ◎2-14

① Batteries, / particularly rechargeable ones, / are essential / in our daily lives. // ② What technological advances have been made / in the history of batteries? //

1 ③ Batteries are now a large part / of our lives. // ④ They are at the heart of everyday mobile devices, / such as smartphones, / tablets / and laptop computers. // ⑤ Hybrid and electric cars would not exist / without powerful batteries. // ⑥ Innovations in batteries / have had a great impact / on the success of new technologies. //

2 ⑦ Good rechargeable batteries are necessary / in order to make efficient use / of renewable energy sources, / such as sunlight and wind. // ⑧ These energy sources depend highly / on the weather, / and they may not be able / to produce enough electricity / when it is most needed. // ⑨ This is when batteries come into play: / they store electricity / until it is needed. //

3 ⑩ Rechargeable batteries / can contribute to saving the environment. // ⑪ Currently, / single-use primary batteries occupy / most of the market. // ⑫ They are used / only once / and are then thrown away. // ⑬ Billions of such batteries become waste / every year, / and most of them end up in landfills. // ⑭ In contrast, / rechargeable batteries can be reused / many times, / and this lessens / the waste problem of primary batteries. // ⑮ Rechargeable batteries are becoming more important / as a means / to achieve a sustainable, / greener future. //

◁意味のまとまりに注意して，本文全体を音読しよう。（203 Words）

Words and Phrases	新出単語・表現の意味を調べよう		
technological 形 [tèknəlá(:)dʒɪk(ə)l] B1	1.	mobile 形 [móʊb(ə)l] A2	2.
tablet 名 [tǽblət] B1	3.	laptop 形 [lǽptà(:)p]	4.
hybrid 形 [háɪbrɪd] B2	5.	electric 形 [ɪléktrɪk] A2	6.
exist 動 [ɪgzíst] A2	7.	innovation 名 [ìnəvéɪʃ(ə)n] B2	8.
impact 名 [ímpækt] A2	9.	have an impact on …	10.
efficient 形 [ɪfíʃ(ə)nt] B1	11.	come into play	12.
currently 副 [kə́:r(ə)ntli] B1	13.	primary 形 [práɪmèri] B2	14.

occupy 動[á(:)kjəpàɪ] B1	15.	billions of …	16.
in contrast	17.	lessen 動[lés(ə)n] B1	18.
means 名[míːnz] B2	19.		

A 【Comprehension 1】 Fill in the blanks in Japanese.

パラグラフごとの要点を整理しよう【思考力・判断力・表現力】

1	電池は，今や私たちの生活の大きな部分を占めている。スマホなどの（1.　　　　　）の中心にあり，ハイブリッド車や電気自動車にも使われている。
2	太陽光や風などの（2.　　　　）エネルギー源を効率よく利用するためには，性能のよい（3.　　　　　）電池が必要。天候に依存する（2.　　　　　）エネルギーでは必要なときに電気が得られない可能性があり，電気を蓄える必要があるため。
3	（3.　　　　　）電池は環境を守ることに貢献できる。現在，使い捨ての一次電池が市場の主流だが，（4.　　　　）問題がある。対照的に，（3.　　　　）電池は繰り返し使えるので，（4.　　　　）を減らし，環境に優しい。

B 【Comprehension 2】 Answer the following questions in English.

本文のポイントについて答えよう【思考力・判断力・表現力】

1. What have innovations in batteries had a great impact on?

....

2. Why may renewable energy sources not be able to produce enough electricity?

....

3. After single-use primary batteries are used up, what will happen to them?

....

C 【Key Sentences】 Fill in the blank and translate the following sentences.

重要文について確認しよう【知識・技能】【思考力・判断力・表現力】

⑤ Hybrid and electric cars **would** not exist **without** powerful batteries.

◆if … を使わない仮定法。without の句が仮定法の条件を表す。

訳: ....

⑨ This is when batteries come into play: they store electricity until it is needed.

◆コロン（:）は主文に補足説明を加えるために使われている。「すなわち，つまり」などの意味。

◆動詞 store は「…を（1.　　　　　　[日本語で]）」の意味。

訳: ....

77

Part 3 教科書 p.126～p.127 ◀意味のまとまりに注意して，本文全体を聞こう。 ⦿2-16

④ ①What does a typical battery consist of? // ②It has two electrical ends / and a chemical between them. // ③These parts react with each other / inside the battery. // ④As a result, / electricity is produced. // ⑤Many different chemicals can be used / in batteries / and, generally speaking, / they determine a battery's power. //

⑤ ⑥The word "battery" / goes back to the 18th century. // ⑦It was first used / by Benjamin Franklin / of the U.S. // ⑧He called a device / he invented / an "electrical battery." // ⑨It could only store electricity. // ⑩In 1800, / Alessandro Volta of Italy / developed a "true" battery. // ⑪He used copper, / zinc / and salt water / in his device, / and his battery could produce electricity / chemically. // ⑫However, / it couldn't recharge / for reuse. //

⑥ ⑬The earliest rechargeable battery was / the lead-acid battery. // ⑭It was invented / in 1859. // ⑮This type is still widely used / in cars. // ⑯In 1899, / nickel-cadmium batteries were created, / and they were a top choice / for use in portable devices / for many years. // ⑰In the 1990s, / nickel-metal hydride batteries took over. // ⑱They had a longer life. // ⑲They were also less harmful / to the environment. // ⑳Later, / as people wanted smaller and better batteries, / lithium-ion batteries were developed. //

◀意味のまとまりに注意して，本文全体を音読しよう。（188 Words）

Words and Phrases	新出単語・表現の意味を調べよう		
consist 動 [kənsíst] A2	1.	consist of ...	2.
electrical 形 [ɪléktrɪk(ə)l] B1	3.	chemical 名 [kémɪk(ə)l] B1	4.
react 動 [riǽkt] B1	5.	react with ...	6.
Benjamin Franklin [bén(d)ʒ(ə)mɪn frǽŋklɪn]	ベンジャミン・フランクリン	Alessandro Volta [æləsǽndroʊ vóʊltə]	アレッサンドロ・ヴォルタ
copper 名 [kɑ́(:)pər] B2	7.	zinc 名 [zíŋk]	8.
chemically 副 [kémɪk(ə)li]	9.	recharge 動 [rìːtʃɑ́ːrdʒ]	10.
lead 名 [léd]	11.	acid 名 [ǽsɪd] B2	12.
nickel 名 [ník(ə)l]	13.	cadmium 名 [kǽdmiəm]	14.

metal 名[mét(ə)l] A2	15.	hydride 名[háɪdraɪd]	16.
take over	17.	harmful 形[háːrmf(ə)l] A2	18.
be harmful to …	19.	lithium 名[líθiəm]	20.
ion 名[áɪən]	21.		

A 【Comprehension 1】 Fill in the blanks in Japanese.

パラグラフごとの要点を整理しよう【思考力・判断力・表現力】

4	典型的な電池の構造
2つの電極とその間に (₁.　　　　　) があり, それが (₂.　　) し合うことで電気が生まれる。	
5	「電池（バッテリー）」という言葉とその発明
18世紀, ベンジャミン・フランクリンが「電池」を発明。 1800年, アレッサンドロ・ヴォルタが「本当の」電池を開発。	
6	充電式の電池
(₃.　　　　　) 年, 最も古い充電式電池である鉛蓄電池が発明される。 (₄.　　　　　) 年, ニッケルカドミウム電池の開発。 (₅.　　　　　) 年代, ニッケル水素電池の開発。	

B 【Comprehension 2】 Answer the following questions in English.

本文のポイントについて答えよう【思考力・判断力・表現力】

1. How is electricity produced inside a typical battery?

2. What could an "electrical battery" invented by Benjamin Franklin do?

C 【Key Sentences】 Fill in the blank and translate the following sentences.

重要文について確認しよう【知識・技能】【思考力・判断力・表現力】

⑤ Many different chemicals can be used in batteries and, **generally speaking**, they determine a battery's power.

◆generally speaking は「(₁.　　　　　　　　　[日本語で])」の意味。分詞の意味上の主語が主節の主語と必ずしも一致しておらず, 独立した形で慣用的に用いられる独立分詞構文。

訳：

⑥ The word "battery" goes back to the 18th century.

◆go back to … 「…にまでさかのぼる」。「時間的順序」の展開をこの後に続く文で示している。

訳：

Part 4 教科書 p.130～p.131 ◀意味のまとまりに注意して，本文全体を聞こう。 ◎ 2-18

⑦ ①The 2019 Nobel Prize in Chemistry / went to Japanese scientist / Akira Yoshino. // ②He shared the prize / with John B. Goodenough / of the U.S. / and Britain's Stanley Whittingham. // ③They were recognized / for their work / on the lithium-ion battery / (LIB). // ④Yoshino made the battery safe / and commercially usable / for the first time. //

⑧ ⑤The lithium-based battery was invented / by Whittingham / in the 1970s. // ⑥However, / his battery did not last / very long. // ⑦To make matters worse, / it also had a serious safety concern, / as it could catch fire and explode. // ⑧In the 1980s, / a more powerful type was developed / by Goodenough. // ⑨He used lithium-cobalt oxide / on one end of the battery. // ⑩Some years later, / Yoshino made a step / further. // ⑪He adopted Goodenough's idea, / but he used carbon / on the other end. // ⑫This cleared the way / for a safe, / stable / and practical LIB. //

⑨ ⑬The LIB is one of the most common batteries / today. // ⑭Its evolution does not stop, / and many important discoveries / continue to be made. // ⑮Lithium-ion technology is / still full of unknowns / and possibilities. // ⑯Yoshino believes / that the LIB can play a central role / in creating a society / without fossil fuels. // ⑰LIB technology is bringing / great power to people / around the world. //

◀意味のまとまりに注意して，本文全体を音読しよう。(198 Words)

Words and Phrases 新出単語・表現の意味を調べよう			
chemistry 图[kémɪstri] B1	1.	John B. Goodenough [dʒá(:)n bí: gúdɪnʌf]	ジョン B. グッドイナフ
Stanley Whittingham [stǽnli (h)wítɪŋəm]	スタンリー・ウィッティンガム	commercially 副 [kəmə́:rʃ(ə)li]	2.
usable 形[júːzəb(ə)l]	3.	catch fire	4.
explode 動[ɪksplóʊd] B2	5.	cobalt 图[kóʊbɔːlt]	6.
oxide 图[á(:)ksaɪd]	7.	make a step	8.
adopt 動[ədá(:)pt] B1	9.	clear the way for …	10.

| stable 形[stéɪb(ə)l] B1 | 11. | unknown 名[ʌnnóun] | 12. |
| possibility 名 [pὰ(:)səbíləti] B1 | 13. | | |

A 【Comprehension 1】 Fill in the blanks in Japanese.

パラグラフごとの要点を整理しよう【思考力・判断力・表現力】

7	2019年ノーベル（1.　　　　　）賞は，日本の吉野彰博士，アメリカのジョン・B.グッドイナフ博士，イギリスのスタンリー・ウィッティンガム博士が（2.　　　　　　　　）の開発で受賞。
8	（3.　　）年代，ウィッティンガム博士がリチウムを使用した電池を発明。だが安全上の問題があった。 （4.　　）年代，グッドイナフ博士がより強力なタイプを開発。 その数年後，吉野博士が研究を進め，安全で安定した（5.　　　）な（2.　　　　　　　　）を開発。
9	（2.　　　　　　　　）は現在最も一般的な電池の一つであり，その進化は止まることとはない。

B 【Comprehension 2】 Answer the following questions in English.

重要文について確認しよう【知識・技能】【思考力・判断力・表現力】

1. What were the winners of the 2019 Nobel Prize in Chemistry recognized for?

2. What were the problems of Whittingham's lithium-based battery?

3. What does Yoshino believe that the LIB can do?

C 【Key Sentences】 Fill in the blanks and translate the following sentences.

重要文について確認しよう【知識・技能】【思考力・判断力・表現力】

④ Yoshino made the battery safe and commercially usable for the first time.
（S V O C）
◆S＋V＋O＋Cの第5文型。補語は（1.　　　[英語で]）と（2.　　　[英語で]）。
訳：

⑦ **To make matters worse**, it also had a serious safety concern, as it **could** catch fire and explode.
◆to make matters worse は「（3.　　　　　[日本語で]）」の意味。to-不定詞の意味上の主語が主節の主語と必ずしも一致しておらず，独立した形で慣用的に用いられる独立不定詞の文。
◆as it could catch fire and explode の could は「可能性」を表す can の過去形。
訳：

81

Activity Plus 教科書 p.134〜p.135 🔊意味のまとまりに注意して，本文全体を聞こう。 ⊚2-20

①You are listening / to Akira Yoshino speaking / shortly after the announcement / of his Nobel Prize / in Chemistry. //

Q1: ②How did you feel / when you heard / you were awarded / the prize? //

③I couldn't believe the news, / and it didn't feel real / at first. // ④On the phone, / I had an interview / in English. // ⑤Actually, / I felt uneasy / about it / because I thought my English interview / would be broadcast / around the world. //

Q2: ⑥How can the lithium-ion battery help / a society / based on renewable energy? //

⑦I believe / lithium-ion batteries in electric cars / can help greatly. // ⑧Our future society needs / a better power storage system. // ⑨If electric cars become widespread, / they can compose / a huge power storage system. // ⑩That will stimulate / the use of solar and wind power. //

Q3: ⑪What message do you have / for young people / who are interested / in science? //

⑫You should look for and nourish / a seed of interest. // ⑬In my case, / it was a book / about candles. // ⑭When I read it, / I thought / chemistry was fascinating. // ⑮That experience / has led to my work / on the lithium-ion battery. // ⑯When you get interested / in something / and work toward it, / you will become better / at it. //

🔊意味のまとまりに注意して，本文全体を音読しよう。（190 Words）

Words 新出単語の意味を調べよう			
uneasy 形 [ʌníːzi] A2	1.	broadcast 動 [brɔ́ːdkæst] B2	2.
widespread 形 [wáɪdsprèd] B1	3.	compose 動 [kəmpóʊz] B1	4.
stimulate 動 [stímjəlèɪt] B2	5.	nourish 動 [nə́ːrɪʃ] B2	6.
candle 名 [kǽnd(ə)l] B1	7.		

A 【Comprehension 1】 Fill in the blanks in Japanese.

要点を整理しよう【思考力・判断力・表現力】

ノーベル化学賞受賞発表直後の吉野彰さんの話

Q1：受賞の知らせを聞いたときの気持ちは？
最初は信じられず，現実だと感じなかった。 電話で受けた英語のインタビューが世界中に放送されると思い，（1.　　　）に感じていた。
Q2：リチウムイオン電池は再生可能エネルギー社会にどのように役立つか？
（2.　　　　　　）が普及すれば，巨大な電力（3.　　　　　）システムを構成することができる。そうすれば，太陽光発電や風力発電の利用も活性化されるだろう。
Q3：科学に興味を持つ若い人たちへのメッセージ
（4.　　　　　）の種を探し，育てていくことが大切だ。私はロウソクについての本を読み， （5.　　　　　）は魅力的だと思った。

B 【Comprehension 2】 Answer the following questions in English.

本文のポイントについて答えよう【思考力・判断力・表現力】

1. Why did Yoshino feel uneasy about having an interview in English?

----

2. What does our future society need?

----

3. What is Yoshino's advice for young people who are interested in science?

C 【Key Sentences】 Fill in the blanks and translate the following sentences.

重要文について確認しよう【知識・技能】【思考力・判断力・表現力】

① <u>You</u> <u>are listening to</u> <u>Akira Yoshino</u> <u>speaking</u> shortly after the announcement of his Nobel Prize in Chemistry.

◆知覚動詞 listen to＋O＋現在分詞「O が〜しているのを聞く」。

訳:---

⑦ I **believe** lithium-ion batteries in electric cars can help greatly.

◆I believe の後の that が省略されている。that-節中の主語は（1.　　　　　[英語 2 語で]），
動詞は can（2.　　　　　[英語で]）。

訳:---

Part 1 教科書 p.140~p.141 🔊意味のまとまりに注意して，本文全体を聞こう。 ◉2-22

① You are reading / a blog post / about a famous tree / in Hokkaido / which was very popular / among tourists. //

② I have to tell you / a very disappointing thing. // ③ Unfortunately, / a famous tree on a farm / in Biei, / Hokkaido, / was finally cut down / by the landowner. // ④ This tree, / leaning far to one side / in the middle of a field, / resembled a philosopher / in deep thought. // ⑤ That is why / it came to be called / the "Philosophy Tree." //

⑥ Occasionally, / the owner could not work / on his farm / because of tourists / blocking the road / with their parked cars. // ⑦ More and more tourists entered / his private land / to get the best shots / on their smartphones, / and they damaged his crops. // ⑧ They ignored warning signs / saying, / "PRIVATE PROPERTY: / NO ENTRY." // ⑨ The signs were written / not only in Japanese and English / but also in Chinese and Korean. //

⑩ I, / and maybe other people / in Japan, / too, / felt a sense of crisis. // ⑪ On behalf of the bloggers / in Japan, / I wrote about it / on this blog. // ⑫ In the end, / the worst result has come about / and I am shocked. // ⑬ I am afraid / that similar incidents with tourists / may happen / in other popular areas / in the future. // ⑭ What can we do / to prevent this? // ⑮ What measures / should we take? //

🔊意味のまとまりに注意して，本文全体を音読しよう。 (208 Words)

Words and Phrases 新出単語・表現の意味を調べよう			
unfortunately 副 [ʌ̀nfɔ́ːrtʃ(ə)nətli] A2	1.	landowner 名 [lǽndòʊnər]	2.
lean 動 [liːn] B2	3.	lean to …	4.
in the middle of …	5.	resemble 動 [rɪzémb(ə)l] B1	6.
philosopher 名 [fəlá(ː)səfər] B1	7.	occasionally 副 [əkéɪʒ(ə)n(ə)li] B1	8.
block A with B	9.	private 形 [práɪvət] A2	10.
warning 形 [wɔ́ːrnɪŋ]	11.	crisis 名 [kráɪsɪs] B1	12.

behalf 名[bɪháef] B1	13.	on behalf of …	14.
blogger 名[blάːgər] B1	15.	in the end	16.
come about	17.	incident 名[ínsɪd(ə)nt] B1	18.
measure 名[méʒər] B1	19.	take measures	20.

A 【Comprehension 1】 Fill in the blanks in Japanese.

要点を整理しよう【思考力・判断力・表現力】

北海道・美瑛 の農場に「(1.　　　　　)の木」と呼ばれる木があった。
➡農地の真ん中で片側に傾く姿が思案する哲学者に似ていた。
　土地の所有者はその木を（2.　　　　　）した。
原因：土地の所有者が観光客に困っていたため。
　➡（3.　　　）で道をふさいだり，スマホで（4.　　　　　）をす
　るために私有地に立ち入ったりする。
対策：立ち入り禁止の看板を（5.　　　）か国語で書いて立てた。
　➡無視された。

B 【Comprehension 2】 Answer the following questions in English.

本文のポイントについて答えよう【思考力・判断力・表現力】

1. Why does the blogger feel disappointed?

----

2. Why was the tree in Biei called the "Philosophy Tree"?

C 【Key Sentences】 Fill in the blanks and translate the following sentences.

重要文について確認しよう【知識・技能】【思考力・判断力・表現力】

④ **This tree**, leaning far to one side in the middle of a field, resembled
a philosopher in deep thought.

　◆ This tree＝(1.　　　　　　　　　　　　　　　　　[日本語で])
　◆主語と動詞の間に分詞構文が挿入されている。resemble は他動詞で，目的語をともなう。
　訳: --

⑤ **That is why** it **came to** be called the "Philosophy Tree."

　◆ that is why … 「そういうわけで…」。why は関係副詞で，the reason why … の意味。
　◆ come to ～は「(2.　　　　　　　　　　　　　　　[日本語で])」の意味。
　訳: --

Part 2 教科書 p.142〜p.143 📣意味のまとまりに注意して，本文全体を聞こう。 ◎2-24

①Do you want / to travel abroad? // ②With a restriction on non-essential travel / and complete lockdown / in some countries, / we were able to witness / what could happen / to the world. //

1 ③Recently, / tourism has gone through some decline / due to infectious diseases / and natural disasters. // ④In fact, / it is still fresh / in our memory / that the number of tourists decreased drastically / in 2020 / due to the influence of COVID-19. // ⑤However, / do you remember / that tourists were visiting various spots / in large numbers / at one time? //

2 ⑥Overtourism quickly became / one of the most serious social problems / in the modern age of travel. // ⑦More and more people visited sightseeing places, / thanks to cheaper air fares, / rising incomes / and the power of social media. // ⑧These places were no longer able / to cope with their own popularity. // ⑨In the past few years, / a number of destinations have raised the alarm / over this situation. //

3 ⑩In 2018, / the Oxford Dictionary chose "overtourism" / as one of its Words of the Year. // ⑪The World Tourism Organization defined it / as "the negative impact / that tourism has / on a destination." // ⑫An excess of tourist crowds impacted / the local people's quality of life. // ⑬Excessive crowds hindered the experiences / of the tourists themselves. // ⑭Many places / dependent on money from tourism wondered / if they could maintain a good environment / not only for travelers / but also for their own residents. //

📣意味のまとまりに注意して，本文全体を音読しよう。（224 Words）

Words and Phrases 新出単語・表現の意味を調べよう			
restriction 名 [rɪstríkʃ(ə)n] B2	1.	lockdown 名[lá(:)kdàun]	2.
tourism 名[túərìz(ə)m] B1	3.	decline 名[dɪkláɪn] B1	4.
infectious 形 [ɪnfékʃəs] B2	5.	drastically 副[dræstɪkəli]	6.
COVID-19 [kóʊvɪd nàɪntíːn]	コヴィッド19	at one time	7.
overtourism 名 [òʊvərtúərìz(ə)m]	8.	fare 名[féər] A2	9.
cope 動[kóʊp] B2	10.	cope with …	11.
destination 名 [dèstɪnéɪʃ(ə)n] B1	12.	alarm 名[əláːrm] A2	13.

raise the alarm	14.	Oxford [ά(:)ksfərd]	オックスフォード
crowd 名[kráud] A2	15.	excessive 形 [ɪksésɪv] B2	16.
hinder 動[híndər]	17.	dependent 形 [dɪpénd(ə)nt] B1	18.
be dependent on …	19.	resident 名[rézɪd(ə)nt] B2	20.

A 【Comprehension 1】 Fill in the blanks in Japanese.

パラグラフごとの要点を整理しよう【思考力・判断力・表現力】

2018年	観光客の増え過ぎが深刻な社会問題となっていた。 理由 (1.　　　　　　　　) の安さ, (2.　　　　　　) の増加, SNS の普及。 観光地では, 観光客の増え過ぎに対処できなくなっていた。
	オーバーツーリズムという言葉がオックスフォードの「その年の言葉」の1つに選ばれた。 定義 旅行業が目的地［観光地］に与える (3.　　　　　　) 影響。
2020年	(4.　　　　　　　　) の影響で, 観光客が急激に減少

B 【Comprehension 2】 Answer the following questions in English.

本文のポイントについて答えよう【思考力・判断力・表現力】

1. Why did tourism decline in 2020?

　--

2. What did the World Tourism Organization define "overtourism" as?

　--

C 【Key Sentences】 Fill in the blanks and translate the following sentences.

重要文について確認しよう【知識・技能】【思考力・判断力・表現力】

③ Recently, tourism has **gone through** some decline **due to** infectious diseases and natural disasters.

◆ go through … は「…を (1.　　　　　[日本語で])」, due to … は「…の (2.　　　　　[日本語で])」の意味。

訳 : --

⑭ Many places (dependent on money from tourism) wondered if they could maintain a good environment.

◆ dependent on … は形容詞の後置修飾。形容詞がほかの語句をともなって名詞を修飾する場合は, 名詞の後に置かれる。

◆ wonder if … 「…ではないかと思う」。if-節全体が目的語となっている。

訳 : --

Part 3 教科書 p.144〜p.145 🔊意味のまとまりに注意して，本文全体を聞こう。 💿2-26

④ ①At one time, / overtourism was making headlines / all over the world. // ②In Barcelona, / residents protested against many problems / caused by having too many tourists. // ③In Paris, / workers at the Louvre Museum / went on strike over dangerous conditions / resulting from having too many visitors. // ④In Venice, / residents tried hard / to get cruise ships banned / from docking there. // ⑤On Mt. Everest, / some climbers have died of altitude sickness / because of the delays / caused by too many climbers. //

⑤ ⑥How about in Japan? // ⑦The number of tourists / coming to this country / was once increasing rapidly. // ⑧Inbound tourism contributed greatly / to the Japanese economy. // ⑨Having too many visitors, / however, / can lead to many problems, / such as noise, / litter / and traffic congestion. // ⑩It can cause great inconvenience / to local residents. // ⑪It may even spoil the attraction / of the sightseeing spot itself. //

⑥ ⑫In Kyoto, / people were feeling the negative impacts / of overtourism. // ⑬For example, / they had trouble boarding the buses / by which they commute. // ⑭One of the local residents expressed his mixed feelings: / "Many locals depend on tourism, / so I'm not saying we don't need tourists. // ⑮But / we do see / its negative impacts." // ⑯Even Japanese tourists avoided visiting Kyoto / because of overtourism. // 🔊意味のまとまりに注意して，本文全体を音読しよう。(195 Words)

Words and Phrases 新出単語・表現の意味を調べよう			
headline 名[hédlàin] B1	1.	Barcelona [bà:rsəlóunə]	バルセロナ
Louvre [lú:vr(ə)]	ルーブル	strike 名[stráik] A2	2.
go on strike	3.	result from …	4.
Venice [vénis]	ベニス	cruise 名[krú:z] A2	5.
ban 動[bǽn] B2	6.	ban A from B	7.
dock 動[dá(:)k]	8.	climber 名[kláimər] B1	9.
altitude 名[ǽltitjù:d] B2	10.	sickness 名[síknəs] B1	11.
delay 名[diléi] A2	12.	inbound 形[ínbàund]	13.

congestion 名 [kəndʒéstʃ(ə)n]	14.	inconvenience 名 [ìnkənví:niəns]	15.
attraction 名 [ətrǽkʃ(ə)n] B1	16.	have trouble ～ing	17.
commute 動 [kəmjú:t] B2	18.		

A 【Comprehension 1】 Fill in the blanks in Japanese.

パラグラフごとの要点を整理しよう【思考力・判断力・表現力】

①バルセロナ　観光客の問題に（1.　　　　）が抗議した。

②パリ　　　ルーブル美術館で働く人が（2.　　　　）をした。

③ベニス　　巡行船の（3.　　　　）を禁止しようとした。

④エベレスト　過密による遅延により，（4.　　　　）で死亡する登山家がいる。

⑤京都　　　（5.　　　　）のためバスに乗るときの問題もあり，住民は複雑な気持ちになっている。

B 【Comprehension 2】 Answer the following questions in English.

本文のポイントについて答えよう【思考力・判断力・表現力】

1. What did residents in Barcelona protest against?

2. What contributed greatly to the Japanese economy?

3. Why did some Japanese tourists avoid visiting Kyoto?

C 【Key Sentences】 Translate the following sentences.

重要文について確認しよう【知識・技能】【思考力・判断力・表現力】

③ Workers went on strike over dangerous conditions (resulting from having too many visitors).

◆ resulting は現在分詞で，dangerous conditions を修飾している。

訳：

⑬ For example, they had trouble boarding the buses **by which** they commute.

◆関係詞節の中で関係詞が前置詞の目的語になる場合がある。〈先行詞＋前置詞＋関係詞〉の語順になる。commute by the buses「バスで通勤する」の，the buses が先行詞になった形。

訳：

89

Part 4 教科書 p.148 意味のまとまりに注意して，本文全体を聞こう。 ⊙2-28

7 ①Now is the time / when we should reflect on / what it actually means / to travel. // ②Imagine / that you are a resident / of a famous tourist destination. // ③Do you think / people in your town want / to welcome more tourists / from abroad? // ④Do you think / foreign tourists / who visit your town / will come back again / in the future? //

8 ⑤Professor Harold Goodwin, / who wrote *Responsible Tourism*, / remarked, / "Tourism is like a fire / —— you can use it / to cook your food / or it can burn your house down." // ⑥Responsible tourism is about making places better / for people to live in / and better for people to visit. // ⑦It demands responsibility / for achieving sustainable development. //

9 ⑧How can we achieve responsible tourism / to overcome the problems of overtourism? // ⑨There is no single perfect solution / to these problems. // ⑩There are, / however, / many ways to reduce crowding / and protect the environment. // ⑪It is by taking a more responsible approach / to tourism / that we can maximize the positive effects / and minimize the negative ones. // ⑫We all live / on this beautiful planet / and we are in the same boat. // ⑬Traveling should be a beneficial experience. // ⑭It is up to us / to make sure / it stays that way. //

意味のまとまりに注意して，本文全体を音読しよう。（197 Words）

Words and Phrases	新出単語・表現の意味を調べよう		
professor 图[prəfésər] B1	1.	Harold Goodwin [hǽr(ə)ld gúdwɪn]	ハロルド・グッドウィン
responsible 形 [rɪspá(ː)nsəb(ə)l] B1	2.	remark 動[rɪmáːrk] B1	3.
burn ... down	4.	demand 動[dɪmǽnd] B1	5.
maximize 動[mǽksɪmàɪz]	6.	minimize 動[mínɪmàɪz] B1	7.
beneficial 形 [bènɪfíʃ(ə)l] B2	8.		

A 【**Comprehension 1**】 Fill in the blanks in Japanese.

パラグラフごとの要点を整理しよう【思考力・判断力・表現力】

責任ある観光：オーバーツーリズムを克服するための新しい旅行様式
・（1. ＿＿＿＿＿＿＿）にとっても，訪れる人にとってもその場所をよりよくする。
・持続可能な開発を達成するための（2. ＿＿＿＿）を必要とする。
どのように責任ある観光は達成されるか。
・オーバーツーリズムを解決する完璧な方法はないが，（3. ＿＿＿＿）を減らしたり，環境を保護したりすることができる。
・旅行により責任を持って臨むことで，旅行のよい影響を最大限に引き出し，（4. ＿＿＿＿）を最小限に抑える。
・旅行とは有益な経験であるべきだ。

B 【**Comprehension 2**】 Answer the following questions in English.

本文のポイントについて答えよう【思考力・判断力・表現力】

1. Who is Harold Goodwin?

   ....

2. What does responsible tourism demand?

   ....

3. According to the writer, what should traveling be?

   ....

C 【**Key Sentences**】 Fill in the blanks and translate the following sentences.

重要文について確認しよう【知識・技能】【思考力・判断力・表現力】

① Now is the time (**when** we should **reflect on** what it actually means to travel).
   ◆ the time を関係副詞 when の節が修飾している。
   ◆ reflect on ... は「…を（1. ＿＿＿＿ [日本語で]）」の意味。
   ◆ on の目的語は what の節。it は形式主語で，真主語は（2. ＿＿＿＿＿＿＿ [英語 2 語で]）。
   訳 : ....

⑧ How can we achieve responsible tourism **to overcome** the problems of overtourism?
   ◆ we を用いた疑問文で読者を巻き込んだ質問を投げかけ，文章全体の結論のパラグラフを始めている。
   ◆ to overcome は副詞用法で，動詞 achieve の目的を示している。
   訳 : ....

⑪ **It is** by taking a more responsible approach to tourism **that** we can maximize the positive effects and minimize the negative ones.
   ◆強調構文は it is の後ろに置いた語句を強調する。ここでは前置詞句を強調している。
   ◆強調構文を使わずに書きかえると We can maximize the positive effects and minimize the negative ones by taking a more responsible approach to tourism.。ones＝（3. ＿＿＿＿ [英語で]）。
   訳 : ....

Activity Plus 教科書 p.152～p.153 意味のまとまりに注意して，本文全体を聞こう。 2-30

①In your class, / you are listening / to a discussion / of the following statement: / "In order to prevent overtourism, / people should not post pictures / of their trips / on social media." //

Teacher: ②As we have learned, / overtourism has become a crucial problem / in many places. // ③When people make a decision / about where to visit and when, / they depend greatly on the information / they see / on social media. // ④So / for today's discussion, / let's talk about the statement, / "In order to prevent overtourism, / people should not post pictures / of their trips / on social media." // ⑤What's your opinion, / Satoshi? //

Satoshi: ⑥Frankly, / I disagree / with this statement. // ⑦Many people want / to travel for the purpose / of taking great pictures / and showing them online. // ⑧I think / it's a good thing. // ⑨If you don't get hundreds of likes / on your posts, / is it even worth going? // ⑩If you don't have / any good pictures / to post on social media, / will you still go traveling? // ⑪I wouldn't. // ⑫How about you, / Emily? //

Emily: ⑬Well, / I'm afraid / that traveling has become a photo contest / for many tourists. // ⑭Wherever I travel, / I see the growing trend of / "doing it for social media." // ⑮It's all about who can get the best shots, / and it's all evaluated / by the number of likes and followers / you have. // ⑯So / I agree / with this statement. // ⑰Now, / it's your turn, / Mika. //

Mika: ⑱My idea is different / from Emily's. // ⑲I believe / that social media can contribute / to helping with "undertourism." // ⑳That is the movement / for attracting people / to less-visited places / that need more attention. // ㉑Plus, / I think / social media are not the only reason / for overtourism. // ㉒In conclusion, / I don't agree / with this statement. //

意味のまとまりに注意して，本文全体を音読しよう。(270 Words)

Words and Phrases 新出単語・表現の意味を調べよう			
statement 名 [stéɪtmənt] A2	1.	crucial 形 [krúːʃ(ə)l] B2	2.
frankly 副 [frǽŋkli] B2	3.	disagree with …	4.
for the purpose of …	5.	worth 前 [wɔ́ːrθ] B1	6.

be worth ～ing	7.	wherever 接 [(h)weərévər] B1	8.
trend 名 [trénd] B1	9.	undertourism 名 [ˌʌndərtʊ́ərìz(ə)m]	10.
plus 接 [plʌ́s] A2	11.	conclusion 名 [kənklúːʒ(ə)n] B1	12.
in conclusion	13.		

A 【Comprehension 1】 Fill in the blanks in Japanese.

要点を整理しよう【思考力・判断力・表現力】

ディスカッションの命題：旅行で撮影した写真を SNS に投稿すべきでない		
発表者	賛成／反対	理由
サトシ	(1.　　　)	たくさんの人がすばらしい写真を撮って，(2.　　　　　　　　) でそれらを見せたいと思っている。「いいね」をもらえなかったり，SNS に掲載するよい写真がないのなら，旅行に行く意味はあるのか。
エミリー	(3.　　　)	旅行が多くの観光客にとって写真の (4.　　　　　) になっており，どこへ旅行しても「SNS のために旅行する人」を見かける。「いいね」や (5.　　　　　　) の数ですべてが評価される。
ミカ	(6.　　　)	SNS はアンダーツーリズムに貢献することができる。 ➡あまり人が来ず，より注目されたい観光地に人を集める。 また，SNS だけが (7.　　　　　　　　) の理由ではない。

B 【Comprehension 2】 Answer the following questions in English.

本文のポイントについて答えよう【思考力・判断力・表現力】

1. According to Satoshi's opinion, why do many people want to travel?

....

2. What is "undertourism"?

....

C 【Key Sentence】 Fill in the blank and translate the following sentence.

重要文について確認しよう【知識・技能】【思考力・判断力・表現力】

⑭ **Wherever** I travel, I see the growing trend of "**doing it** for social media."

◆ wherever＋S＋V は「S が V するところはどこでも」の意味。

◆ doing it＝(1.　　　　　　[英語で])

訳 : ....

Part 1 教科書 p.158〜p.159 🔊意味のまとまりに注意して，本文全体を聞こう。 💿2-32

①I am sitting / in an overstuffed chair / in the lobby / of The Dominion Imperial International Hotel. // ②No kidding, / that's really the name. // ③My friend Wendy dragged me here / to meet a guy, / but he doesn't know it. // ④In fact, / he's never heard of Wendy. // ⑤But that doesn't stop her / from being in love with him. // ⑥Well, / maybe not in love. // ⑦I think / love is for people / you've at least met. // ⑧Wendy has never met Craig the Cat. // ⑨That's the name of the guy. // ⑩At least / that's his stage name. // ⑪He's a rock star / who's been famous / for over six months. // ⑫Even *my* parents have heard of him. //

⑬Wendy is here / to get Craig the Cat's autograph / on his latest album. // ⑭She constantly talks about Craig the Cat. // ⑮But it was like discussing something / that was going on / in another time frame, / on another continent. // ⑯I didn't mind. // ⑰It was nicely, safely unreal. // ⑱Until Craig the Cat came to town / today. //

⑲Wendy looks at her watch. // ⑳"He's showered / and is relaxing now. // ㉑He's feeling rested, / triumphant, / and receptive." //

㉒"Receptive to what?" //

㉓"To meeting us. // ㉔To autographing *my* album." //

㉕"How are you going to accomplish that? // ㉖You don't actually know / that he's staying at this hotel, / and even if he is, / you don't know his room number." //

㉗Wendy stands up. // ㉘"Don't be so negative, / Rosalind. // ㉙Come," / she says. //

㉚I follow her / to one of those telephones / that connect the caller to hotel rooms. // ㉛She dials a number. // ㉜She waits. // ㉝Then / she says, / "Craig the Cat, / please." //

🔊意味のまとまりに注意して，本文全体を音読しよう。(254 Words)

Words and Phrases	新出単語・表現の意味を調べよう		
overstuffed 形 [òʊvərstʌ́ft]	1.	lobby 名 [lɑ́(:)bi] B2	2.
dominion 名 [dəmínjən]	3.	no kidding	4.
Wendy [wéndi]	ウェンディ	drag 動 [drǽg] B1	5.
hear of …	6.	stop … from 〜ing	7.
at least	8.	autograph 名 [ɔ́:təgræf]	9.

frame 名[fréɪm] A2	10.	unreal 形[ʌnríː(ə)l]	11.
triumphant 形 [traɪʌ́mf(ə)nt]	12.	receptive 形[rɪséptɪv]	13.
be receptive to ...	14.	stand up	15.
Rosalind [rázələnd]	ロザリンド	caller 名[kɔ́ːlər] B1	16.
dial 動[dáɪəl] B1	17.		

A 【Comprehension 1】 Fill in the blanks in Japanese.

要点を整理しよう【思考力・判断力・表現力】

主人公の名前は（1.　　　　　　　）	クレイグ・ザ・キャット
・ホテルの（2.　　　　　）にいる。	・職業は（5.　　　　　　）である。 ・ホテルに滞在していると思われる。
友人の名前は（3.　　　　　　）	
・「クレイグ・ザ・キャット」に夢中。 ・（4.　　　　　）をもらうためにホテルにやってきた。	

B 【Comprehension 2】 Answer the following questions in English.

本文のポイントについて答えよう【思考力・判断力・表現力】

1. Why does Rosalind think that Wendy isn't in love with Craig the Cat?

　--

2. What is Wendy going to do?

　--

C 【Key Sentences】 Fill in the blanks and translate the following sentences.

重要文について確認しよう【知識・技能】【思考力・判断力・表現力】

⑤ **That** doesn't stop her from being in love with him.
　◆ That＝(1.　　　　　　　　　　　　　　　　　　　　[日本語で])。
　訳：--

⑳ He's showered and is relaxing now.　He's feeling receptive."
　◆ He's showered＝He (2.　　[英語で]) showered, He's feeling＝He (3.　　[英語で]) feeling。
　◆ He's receptive＝He's receptive to (4.　　　　[英語で]) Wendy and Rosalind。
　訳：--

Part 2 教科書 p.160〜p.161 ◀意味のまとまりに注意して，本文全体を聞こう。 ◎2-34

①She looks at me. // ②"I found him! // ③Listen!" // ④She turns the receiver / so that I, / too, / can hear. //

⑤A woman is on the other end. // ⑥"How did you find out / where Craig the Cat is staying?" / she asks. // ⑦"The leak. // ⑧I need to know / where the leak is." //

⑨"There isn't any. // ⑩I'm the only one / with the information. // ⑪Please listen. // ⑫I want his autograph." //

⑬"Who doesn't?" //

⑭"Help me / get it, / please. // ⑮What are my chances?" //

⑯"Poor to none." //

⑰"Oh." //

⑱"I'm his manager / and, / my dear, / I'm his mother. // ⑲I protect Craig / from two vantage points. // ⑳Now, / how many other fans know / where he's staying?" //

㉑"None / that I know of." //

㉒"You mean / you didn't sell the information / to the highest bidder?" //

㉓"I wouldn't do that." //

㉔"Maybe not, / dear, / but I'm tired of his fans. // ㉕Leave him alone! // ㉖I'm hanging up." //

㉗Click. //

㉘Wendy sighs. // ㉙"We'll just have to wait / until he goes into that place / over there / to eat." //

㉚"Haven't you ever heard of room service?" //

㉛"Craig doesn't like room service. // ㉜He doesn't like dining rooms, / either. // ㉝He's a coffee shop person." //

㉞"How do you know?" //

㉟"I know." //

㊱"How did you know his room number?" //

㊲"I knew." //   ◀意味のまとまりに注意して，本文全体を音読しよう。 (195 Words)

Words and Phrases 新出単語・表現の意味を調べよう			
receiver 名 [rɪsíːvər]	1.	on the other end	2.

leak 名[líːk] B2	3.	none 代[nʌ́n] B1	4.
vantage 名[vǽntɪdʒ]	5.	know of ...	6.
bidder 名[bídər]	7.	be tired of ...	8.
leave ... alone	9.	hang up	10.
click 名[klík] B1	11.	sigh 動[sáɪ] B2	12.
over there	13.		

A 【**Comprehension 1**】 Fill in the blanks in Japanese.

要点を整理しよう【思考力・判断力・表現力】

ウェンディとロザリンド	クレイグ・ザ・キャット
・クレイグ・ザ・キャットに電話をかける。 ・ウェンディはクレイグの（1.　　　　　）がほしいと伝える。 ・クレイグの（2.　　　　　）をリークしていると疑われるが，否定する。 ・クレイグが（3.　　　　　）をしにくるまで待つことを決める。	 ・電話には出ない。
	クレイグの母親＝クレイグの（4.　　　　　）
	・ウェンディとロザリンドの情報リークを疑う。 ・クレイグの（5.　　　　　）にうんざりしている。 ・ウェンディの電話を切る。

B 【**Comprehension 2**】 Answer the following questions in English.

本文のポイントについて答えよう【思考力・判断力・表現力】

1. Besides Wendy and Rosalind, how many fans know where Craig is staying?

2. After the phone call, what do Wendy and Rosalind decide to do?

C 【**Key Sentence**】 Fill in the blank and translate the following sentence.

重要文について確認しよう【知識・技能】【思考力・判断力・表現力】

⑬ "Who doesn't?"

◆この文は Who doesn't（1.　　　　　　[英語3語で]）? と補うことができる。

◆一種の反語表現で，「だれが〜しないだろうか」 → 「〜しない人などいるものか」 という意味。

訳 :

Part 3 教科書 p.162〜p.163 意味のまとまりに注意して，本文全体を聞こう。 2-36

①We are sitting / in the overstuffed chairs / again. // ②Wendy is watching and waiting. // ③I see no human-size cat / in the lobby. // ④I feel like going to sleep. //

⑤Almost an hour goes by. // ⑥Suddenly, / Wendy pokes me. // ⑦"It's him! // It's him!" //

⑧I look up. // ⑨A guy / who seems to be about twenty or twenty-five / is passing by / with a woman / who looks old enough / to be his mother. // ⑩He is lean. // ⑪She is not. // ⑫They are dressed normally. //

⑬I whisper to Wendy. // ⑭"*That's* Craig the Cat? // ⑮How do you know? // ⑯He looks like an ordinary guy." //

⑰Wendy doesn't answer. // ⑱She stands up / and starts to follow the guy and the woman. // ⑲They are heading / for the hotel coffee shop. // ⑳I follow all of them. // ㉑I see the guy and the woman / sit down. // ㉒They are looking at menus. //

㉓Wendy rushes up to them, / clutching her album. // ㉔"May I have your autograph?" / she asks the guy. //

㉕The woman glares at Wendy. // ㉖"He doesn't give autographs," / she says. // ㉗"He's just an ordinary person. // ㉘Can't you see / he's just an ordinary person?" //

㉙"*You're Craig the Cat!*" // ㉚Wendy says to the guy. //

㉛She says it too loudly. //

㉜"How do you know / I'm Craig the Cat?" / the guy asks. // ㉝Also too loudly. //

㉞People in the coffee shop / turn and stare. // ㉟They repeat, / "Craig the Cat!" //

㊱Suddenly / somebody with a camera appears / and aims the camera at Craig. // ㊲Wendy bends down / and puts her face / in front of Craig's. // ㊳It happens so fast, / I can't believe it. // ㊴The photographer says, / "Get out of the way, / kid." //

意味のまとまりに注意して，本文全体を音読しよう。(259 Words)

Words and Phrases　新出単語・表現の意味を調べよう

feel like …	1.	go by	2.
poke 動[póʊk]	3.	look up	4.
lean 形[líːn] B1	5.	normally 副[nɔ́ːrm(ə)li] B1	6.
whisper 動[(h)wíspər] B2	7.	ordinary 形[ɔ́ːrd(ə)nèri] B1	8.
head for …	9.	rush 動[rʌ́ʃ] B1	10.
clutch 動[klʌ́tʃ]	11.	glare 動[gléər]	12.
stare 動[stéər] B1	13.	aim 動[éɪm] B2	14.
aim A at B	15.	bend 動[bénd] A2	16.
bend down	17.	get out of the way	18.

A 【Comprehension 1】 Fill in the blanks in Japanese.

要点を整理しよう【思考力・判断力・表現力】

ウェンディとロザリンド	クレイグ・ザ・キャット
・ロビーでクレイグを待つ。 ・ウェンディがクレイグを見つけるが，ロザリンドには一般男性にしか見えない。 ・ホテルの（1.　　　　　）に入る。 ・男性に（2.　　　　　）をもらうよう依頼する。 ・男性がクレイグであると気付いた，（3.　　　　　）を持った人からクレイグを守る。	・ホテルの（1.　　　　　）に入る。 ・自分がクレイグであると思わず口走ってしまう。 **クレイグの母親** ・ホテルの（1.　　　　　）に入る。 ・（2.　　　　　）をもらいにきたウェンディをにらみつけ，男性は（4.　　　　　）だと言い張る。

B 【Comprehension 2】 Answer the following questions in English.

本文のポイントについて答えよう【思考力・判断力・表現力】

1. Where in the hotel does Wendy find Craig the Cat?

　
----

2. What does Wendy say to Craig the Cat first?

Part 4 教科書 p.164〜p.165 ◁意味のまとまりに注意して，本文全体を聞こう。 ◉2-38

①Craig's mother glares at the photographer. // ②"Shoo!" / she says, / waving her hand. // ③"Shoo immediately!" //

④The photographer leaves. // ⑤So does Wendy. // ⑥She runs back to me. // ⑦I am hiding / behind a fern. //

⑧Wendy has lost her cool. // ⑨"Let's get out of here / before we're kicked out or arrested," / she says. //

⑩We rush toward a door. //

⑪"Wait!" // ⑫Someone is yelling at us. //

⑬When I hear the word *wait*, / it's a signal / for me to move even faster. // ⑭But Wendy stops. // ⑮"It's *him*!" / she says, / without turning around. //

⑯I turn. // ⑰It *is* Craig the Cat. // ⑱He's alone. // ⑲He rushes up to Wendy. // ⑳"How did you know me?" / he asks. // ㉑"I didn't tell the media / where I was staying. // ㉒And / I certainly didn't give out my room number. // ㉓I wasn't wearing my cat costume. // ㉔And / I was with my mother. // ㉕So *how*?" //

㉖Wendy looks at me. // ㉗She's trying to decide / if she should answer. // ㉘Something in her wants to / and something in her doesn't want to. // ㉙She turns back to Craig. // ㉚"I'm an expert on you," / she says. // ㉛"I know / you like fancy, old hotels, / and this is the oldest and the fanciest in town. // ㉜I know / your lucky number is twelve, / so I figured / you'd stay on the twelfth floor / in room 1212. // ㉝I know / you always wear red socks / when you're not performing, / so tonight / I watched ankles in the lobby. // ㉞And / I knew / you'd be with your manager / —— your mother." //

◁意味のまとまりに注意して，本文全体を音読しよう。（240 Words）

Words and Phrases	新出単語・表現の意味を調べよう		
shoo 間 [ʃúː]	1.	immediately 副 [imíːdiətli] B1	2.
fern 名 [fə́ːrn]	3.	lose one's cool	4.
yell 動 [jél] B2	5.	yell at …	6.
signal 名 [sígn(ə)l] B1	7.	turn around	8.

give out …	9.	costume 名 [kά(:)stʃuːm] B2	10.
fancy 形 [fǽnsi] A2	11.	sock 名 [sά(:)k] A2	12.
ankle 名 [ǽŋk(ə)l] A2	13.		

A 【Comprehension 1】 Fill in the blanks in Japanese.

要点を整理しよう【思考力・判断力・表現力】

ウェンディとロザリンド	クレイグ・ザ・キャット
・たたき出されたり（1.　　　　　　）されるのをおそれて，逃げようとする。 ・クレイグに呼び止められ，足を止める。 ・ウェンディは迷った末，なぜクレイグのことを知っているか説明をする。	・ウェンディとロザリンドを呼び止める。 ・なぜ自分がクレイグ・ザ・キャットとわかったのかたずねる。
➡古い高級ホテルを好む。 ➡ラッキーナンバーは（2.　　　）。 ➡（3.　　）色の靴下をはく。	クレイグの母親 ・（4.　　　　　　）を持った人を追い払う。

B 【Comprehension 2】 Answer the following questions in English.

本文のポイントについて答えよう【思考力・判断力・表現力】

1. Who drove the photographer away?

2. What color are the socks Craig is wearing?

C 【Key Sentences】 Fill in the blanks and translate the following sentences.

重要文について確認しよう【知識・技能】【思考力・判断力・表現力】

④ The photographer leaves. **So does** Wendy.
◆ So で始まる文や節では倒置が起こり，〈So＋V＋S〉で「…もまた～だ」の意味を表す。
◆ does は代動詞。So does Wendy. ＝Wendy (1.　　　　[英語で]), too.
訳:

㉘ Something in her **wants to** and something in her doesn't **want to**.
◆ want to の後には動詞（2.　　　　[英語で]）が省略されている。すでに出てきた動詞を to-不定詞として使うとき，反復を避けるために to だけで表すことがある。この形を代不定詞と呼ぶ。
訳:

Part 5 教科書 p.166～p.167 ◁意味のまとまりに注意して，本文全体を聞こう。 ◎2-40

①"What about the photographer?" //

②"I know / you don't want to be photographed / without your cat costume and makeup. // ③In an interview / on October eighth of this year, / you said / it would wreck your feline image. // ④So / when I saw the photographer / trying to take your picture, / I put my face / in front of yours." //

⑤"You did that for me?" //

⑥"I'd do it / for any special friend." //

⑦"But you don't know me." //

⑧"Yes, I do. // ⑨When I read about someone, / I get to know him. // ⑩I don't believe everything / I read, / of course. // ⑪I pick out certain parts. // ⑫I look for the reality / behind the unreality. // ⑬I went through seventy-one pages / about Craig the Cat, / in eleven different magazines, / and I ended up thinking of you / as my friend." //

⑭Craig the Cat is staring at Wendy / as if *he's* the fan. // ⑮He's in awe of *her*! // ⑯It's nothing very earthshaking. // ⑰It's not like there's a crowd roaring / or it's a summit meeting of world leaders / or a huge change in the universe. // ⑱It's just a small, nice moment / in the lobby of The Dominion Imperial International Hotel, / and it will never go away / for Wendy. //

⑲We're back / in the hotel coffee shop. // ⑳Four of us are sitting around a table, / eating. // ㉑Craig's mother is beaming benevolently / like a contented mother cat / presiding over her brood, / which now includes Wendy and me / in addition to Craig. // ㉒After we finish eating, / Wendy hands her record album to Craig. // ㉓"Now / may I have your autograph?" / she asks. //

◁意味のまとまりに注意して，本文全体を音読しよう。（253 Words）

Words and Phrases 新出単語・表現の意味を調べよう			
makeup 名 [méɪkʌp] A2	1.	wreck 動 [rék]	2.
feline 形 [fíːlaɪn]	3.	pick out …	4.
unreality 名 [ʌnriǽləti]	5.	awe 名 [ɔ́ː] B2	6.
be in awe of …	7.	earthshaking 形 [ɔ́ːrθʃèɪkɪŋ]	8.
roar 動 [rɔ́ːr] B2	9.	universe 名 [júːnɪvə̀ːrs] B1	10.
go away	11.	beam 動 [bíːm]	12.

benevolently 副 [bənév(ə)ləntli]	13.	contented 形 [kənténtɪd]	14.
preside 動 [prɪzáɪd]	15.	preside over …	16.
brood 名 [brúːd]	17.		

A 【Comprehension 1】 Fill in the blanks in Japanese.

ウェンディとロザリンド	クレイグ・ザ・キャット
・ウェンディはなぜ<u>クレイグのこと</u>を知っているか説明をする。	・なぜ自分のことを知り尽くしているかたずねる。
なぜ（1.　　　　）からクレイグを守ったか。 ➡素顔を撮影されると（2.　　　）のようなイメージを台無しにする。	**クレイグの母親**
・ウェンディはクレイグを（3.　　　　）と考えている。	・ウェンディとロザリンドに心を開き，ホテルの（4.　　　　）で食事をする。

B 【Comprehension 2】 Answer the following questions in English.

本文のポイントについて答えよう【思考力・判断力・表現力】

1. Why doesn't Craig want to be photographed without his cat costume and makeup?

---

2. Why is Craig in awe of Wendy?

C 【Key Sentences】 Fill in the blank and translate the following sentences.

重要文について確認しよう【知識・技能】【思考力・判断力・表現力】

⑭ Craig the Cat is staring at Wendy **as if** *he's* the fan.

◆ as if … は（1.　　　　[日本語で]）の意味。as if … の後には仮定法だけでなく直説法も使われる。

訳 : _____

㉑ Craig's mother is beaming benevolently like <u>a contented mother cat</u> (presiding over <u>her brood</u>, (**which** now includes Wendy and me in addition to Craig)).

◆ a contented mother cat が後置の分詞で修飾され，さらにその分詞の句中の名詞が先行詞となり，関係代名詞で説明されている。

訳 : _____

Part 1　教科書 p.174～p.175　◀意味のまとまりに注意して，本文全体を聞こう。◎ 2-42

① When Paul was quite young, / his family had one of the first telephones / in their neighborhood. //

② I remember well the wooden case / fastened to the wall / on the stair landing. // ③ The receiver hung / on the side of the box. // ④ I even remember the number / —— 105. // ⑤ I was too little / to reach the telephone, / but used to listen eagerly / when my mother talked to it. // ⑥ Once / she lifted me up / to speak to my father, / who was away / on business. // ⑦ Magic! //

⑧ Then / I discovered / that somewhere inside that wonderful device / lived an amazing person / —— her name was "Information Please" / and there was nothing / she did not know. //

⑨ My mother could ask her / for anybody's number; / when our clock ran down, / Information Please immediately supplied the correct time. //

⑩ My first personal experience / with this woman-in-the-receiver / came one day / while my mother was visiting a neighbor. // ⑪ Amusing myself / with a hammer, / I hit my finger. // ⑫ The pain was terrible, / but there didn't seem to be much use crying / because there was no one home / to hear me. // ⑬ I walked around the house / sucking my finger, / finally arriving at the landing. // ⑭ The telephone! // ⑮ Quickly / I ran for the footstool / and took it / to the landing. // ⑯ Climbing up, / I took the receiver / and held it to my ear. // ⑰ "Information Please," / I said into the mouthpiece / just above my head. //

◀意味のまとまりに注意して，本文全体を音読しよう。（226 Words）

Words and Phrases　新出単語・表現の意味を調べよう

Paul [pɔ́ːl]	ポール	neighborhood 名 [néɪbərhʊ̀d] B1	1.
wooden 形 [wʊ́d(ə)n] A2	2.	fasten 動 [fǽs(ə)n] B1	3.
fasten A to B	4.	landing 名 [lǽndɪŋ] B2	5.
eagerly 副 [íːgərli] B2	6.	lift 動 [líft] B1	7.
lift ... up	8.	on business	9.
somewhere 副 [sʌ́m(h)wèər] A2	10.	run down	11.

amuse 動 [əmjúːz] B2	12.	amuse A with B	13.
hammer 名 [hǽmər] B1	14.	there is no use ~ing	15.
suck 動 [sʌk] B2	16.	footstool 名 [fútstùːl]	17.
mouthpiece 名 [máʊθpìːs]	18.		

A 【Comprehension 1】 Fill in the blanks in Japanese.

要点を整理しよう【思考力・判断力・表現力】

ポールが幼いとき

住んでいた家の階段の踊り場に（1.　　　　　　）があった。
➡側面に（2.　　　　　）がかかっていた。番号は（3.　　　）であった。
➡中には「インフォメーション・プリーズ」という名の人が住んでいて，何でも知っていた。

インフォメーション・プリーズとの初めての思い出。
➡母親がいないときに（4.　　　　　　）で遊んでいて，指を打ってしまった。
➡（5.　　　　　）を持ってきて受話器を取り，インフォメーション・プリーズに話しかけた。

B 【Comprehension 2】 Answer the following questions in English.

本文のポイントについて答えよう【思考力・判断力・表現力】

1. What was attached to the side of the wooden case?

　　---

2. Why did Paul think there was no use crying when he hit his finger by accident?

C 【Key Sentences】 Fill in the blank and translate the following sentences.

重要文について確認しよう【知識・技能】【思考力・判断力・表現力】

場所や方向を表す副詞句　　　　　V　　　S

⑧ I discovered that [somewhere inside **that wonderful device**] lived an amazing person.
　◆場所や方向を表す副詞句が前に置かれると倒置が起こり，続く部分は V＋S の語順になる。
　◆ that wonderful device＝the（1.　　　　　　　　 [英語2語で]）。
　訳 : ---

⑬ I walked around the house **sucking** my finger, finally **arriving** at the landing.
　◆ sucking, arriving は分詞構文。sucking は「同時」を，arriving は「連続して起こる動作」を表す。
　訳 : ---

105

Part 2 　教科書 p.176〜p.177　　◁意味のまとまりに注意して，本文全体を聞こう。　◎2-44

①A click or two, / and a small, clear voice / spoke into my ear. // ②"Information." //

③"I hurt my fingerrrrr——" / I cried into the phone. // ④The tears began running down, / now that I had an audience. //

⑤"Isn't your mother home?" / came the question. //

⑥"Nobody's home / but me," / I said. //

⑦"Are you bleeding?" //

⑧"No," / I replied. // ⑨"I hit it / with the hammer / and it hurts." //

⑩"Can you open your icebox?" / she asked. // ⑪I said / I could. //

⑫"Then / break off a little piece of ice / and hold it / on your finger. // ⑬That will stop the hurt. // ⑭Be careful / when you use the ice pick," / she warned. // ⑮"And don't cry. // ⑯You'll be all right." //

⑰After that, / I called Information Please / for everything. // ⑱I asked for help / with my geography / and she told me / where Philadelphia was, / and the Orinoco / —— the river / I was going to explore / when I grew up. // ⑲She helped me / with my arithmetic, / and she told me / that a pet chipmunk / —— I had caught him / in the park / just the day before / —— would eat fruit and nuts. //

⑳And / there was the time / that our pet canary died. // ㉑I called Information Please / and told her the sad story. // ㉒She listened, / and then said the usual things / grown-ups say / to soothe a child. // ㉓But I did not feel better: / why should birds sing so beautifully / and bring joy / to whole families, / only to end as a heap of feathers / feet up, / on the bottom of a cage? //

㉔She must have sensed my deep concern, / for she said quietly, / "Paul, / always remember / that there are other worlds / to sing in." //

㉕Somehow / I felt better. //

◁意味のまとまりに注意して，本文全体を音読しよう。(273 Words)

Words and Phrases　新出単語・表現の意味を調べよう			
now that …	1.	reply 動 [rɪpláɪ] B1	2.
icebox 名 [áɪsbà(:)ks]	3.	break off …	4.
geography 名 [dʒiá(:)grəfi] B1	5.	Philadelphia [fìlədélfiə]	フィラデルフィア
Orinoco [ɔ̀:rənóʊkoʊ]	オリノコ川	help A with B	6.

arithmetic 名 [əríθmətìk] B1	7.	chipmunk 名 [tʃípmʌ̀ŋk]	8.
canary 名 [kənéəri]	9.	soothe 動 [súːð] B1	10.
only to ~	11.	heap 名 [híːp] B2	12.
a heap of …	13.	feather 名 [féðər] A2	14.
somehow 副 [sʌ́mhàu] B1	15.		

A 【Comprehension 1】 Fill in the blanks in Japanese.

要点を整理しよう【思考力・判断力・表現力】

ポールが幼いとき
インフォメーション・プリーズに，指をけがしたことを話した。 ➡（1.　　　　）を取り出して，指にあてるように指示を受けた。 その後，さまざまなことをインフォメーション・プリーズにたずねた。 ・（2.　　　　　　）と（3.　　　　　）がどこにあるか ・算数 ・つかまえてきた（4.　　　　　）が食べるもの ペットの（5.　　　　　）が死んだときも電話をかけた。

B 【Comprehension 2】 Answer the following questions in English.

本文のポイントについて答えよう【思考力・判断力・表現力】

1. What did Paul want to explore when he grew up?

   ----

2. What food did Information Please recommend to feed a chipmunk?

C 【Key Sentences】 Fill in the blank and translate the following sentences.

重要文について確認しよう【知識・技能】【思考力・判断力・表現力】

⑳ There was the time (**that** our pet canary died).
   ◆ that を関係副詞のように使うことがある。先行詞は the time。
   訳：--

㉔ She **must have sensed** my deep concern.
   ◆ must have＋過去分詞は「（1.　　　　　　　　　　[日本語で]）」の意味。
   訳：--

Part 3　教科書 p.178～p.179　📣意味のまとまりに注意して，本文全体を聞こう。　💿2-46

① Another day / I was at the telephone. // ② "Information," / said the now familiar voice. //

③ "How do you spell fix?" / I asked. //

④ "Fix something? // ⑤ F-I-X." //

⑥ At that instant / my sister, / trying to scare me, / jumped off the stairs at me. // ⑦ I fell off the footstool, / pulling the receiver / out of the box. // ⑧ We were both terrified / ── Information Please was no longer there, / and I was not at all sure / that I hadn't hurt her / when I pulled the receiver out. //

⑨ Minutes later / there was a man at the door. // ⑩ "I'm a telephone repairman. // ⑪ I was working down the street / and the operator said / there might be some trouble / at this number." // ⑫ He reached for the receiver / in my hand. // ⑬ "What happened?" //

⑭ I told him. //

⑮ "Well, / we can fix that / in a minute or two." // ⑯ He opened the telephone box, / did some repair work, / and then spoke into the phone. // ⑰ "Hi, / this is Pete. // ⑱ Everything's under control / at 105. // ⑲ The kid's sister scared him / and he pulled the cord / out of the box." //

⑳ He hung up, / smiled, / gave me a pat on the head / and walked out of the door. //

㉑ All this took place / in a small town / in the Pacific Northwest. // ㉒ Then, / when I was nine years old, / we moved / across the country to Boston / ── and I missed Information Please / very much. // ㉓ She belonged in that old wooden box back home, / and I somehow never thought of trying the tall, skinny new phone / that sat on a small table / in the hall. //

📣意味のまとまりに注意して，本文全体を音読しよう。（252 Words）

Words and Phrases　新出単語・表現の意味を調べよう			
familiar 形[fəmíljər] A2	1.	instant 名[ínst(ə)nt]	2.
scare 動[skéər] B1	3.	jump off …	4.
fall off …	5.	terrify 動[térəfàɪ] A2	6.

repairman 名 [rɪpéərmæn]	7.	operator 名 [á(:)pərèɪtər] B2	8.
Pete [píːt]	ピート	be under control	9.
cord 名 [kɔ́ːrd]	10.	pat 名 [pæt]	11.
Pacific Northwest [pəsìfɪk nɔ̀ːrθwést]	（北米大陸の）太平洋側北西部	Boston [bɔ́ːst(ə)n]	ボストン
skinny 形 [skíni]	12.		

A 【**Comprehension 1**】 Fill in the blanks in Japanese.

要点を整理しよう【思考力・判断力・表現力】

ポールが幼いとき
姉のいたずらで，（1.　　　　　　　　　　）を引き抜いてしまった。インフォメーション・プリーズの指示を受け，数分後には（2.　　　　　　　　　　）という名の修理工がやってきて，電話を修理していった。
ポールが９歳のとき
家族は（3.　　　　　　）に引っ越した。 ➡そこでは新しい（4.　　　　　　）があったが，なぜか使う気にならなかった。

B 【**Comprehension 2**】 Answer the following questions in English.

本文のポイントについて答えよう【思考力・判断力・表現力】

1. When Paul pulled the receiver out by accident, what did he try to learn?

----

2. How old was Paul when he had to be separated from Information Please?

C 【**Key Sentences**】 Fill in the blanks and translate the following sentences.

重要文について確認しよう【知識・技能】【思考力・判断力・表現力】

⑧ I **was** not at all **sure that** I hadn't hurt her.

◆ be sure that ... は「…を（1.　　　　　　　　[日本語で]）」という意味。形容詞が that-節の場面に対する主語の感情や態度を表す。

◆ not at all は「（2.　　　　　　　　[日本語で]）」という否定の意味。

訳：--

⑳ He hung up, smiled, gave me a pat on the head and walked out of the door.

◆ 4つの動詞（3.　　　　），（4.　　　　），（5.　　　　），（6.　　　[すべて英語で]）が並列されている。

訳：--

Part 4 教科書 p.180～p.181 ◀意味のまとまりに注意して，本文全体を聞こう。◎2-48

①Yet, / as I grew into my teens, / the memories of those childhood conversations / never really left me; / often in moments of doubt and worry / I would recall the serene sense of security / I had / when I knew / that I could call Information Please / and get the right answer. // ②I appreciated now / how patient, understanding and kind she was / to have wasted her time / on a little boy. //

③A few years later, / on my way west to college, / my plane landed in Seattle. // ④I had about half an hour / before my plane left, / and I spent 15 minutes or so / on the phone / with my sister, / who had a happy marriage there now. // ⑤Then, / really without thinking / what I was doing, / I dialed my hometown operator / and said, / "Information Please." //

⑥Miraculously, / I heard again the small, clear voice / I knew so well: / "Information." //

⑦I hadn't planned this, / but I heard myself saying, / "Could you tell me, / please, / how to spell the word 'fix'?" //

⑧There was a long pause. // ⑨Then / came the softly spoken answer. // ⑩"I guess," / said Information Please, / "that your finger must be all right / by now." //

⑪I laughed. // ⑫"So / it's really still you. // ⑬I wonder / if you have any idea / how much you meant to me / during all that time …" //

⑭"I wonder," / she replied, / "if you know / how much you meant to me? // ⑮I never had any children, / and I used to look forward to your calls. // ⑯Silly, / wasn't it?" //   ◀意味のまとまりに注意して，本文全体を音読しよう。(241 Words)

Words and Phrases 新出単語・表現の意味を調べよう			
grow into …	1.	teen 名 [tíːn] B1	2.
doubt 名 [dáut] A2	3.	recall 動 [rikɔ́ːl] B1	4.
serene 形 [səríːn] B2	5.	security 名 [sikjúərəti] B1	6.
appreciate 動 [əpríːʃièit] A2	7.	waste A on B	8.
on one's way to …	9.	… or so	10.
marriage 名 [mǽridʒ] B1	11.	miraculously 副 [mərǽkjələsli]	12.

| pause 名[pɔ́ːz] B1 | 13. | by now | 14. |
| look forward to … | 15. | silly 形[síli] A2 | 16. |

A 【Comprehension 1】 Fill in the blanks in Japanese.

要点を整理しよう【思考力・判断力・表現力】

ポールが10代のとき

インフォメーション・プリーズとの思い出が（1.　　　　　　　）ことはなかった。
インフォメーション・プリーズとは電話口の女性であり，彼女が（2.　　　　　　　），思いやりが
あり，親切に接してくれていたか，このころにはよくわかっていた。

ポールが大学生のとき

飛行機の乗り継ぎの際，シアトルで（3.　　　　　　　）分くらいの空き時間ができた。
姉と15分ほど話した後，故郷の電話交換手に電話をかけた。
　➡幼いときと同じ女性が出た。当時と同じ質問をした。
　➡女性も幼いポールの電話を楽しみにしていた。

B 【Comprehension 2】 Answer the following questions in English.

本文のポイントについて答えよう【思考力・判断力・表現力】

1. When did Paul realize how patient, understanding and kind Information Please was?

　　　　　　　　　　　　　　　　

2. Why did Paul ask how to spell the word "fix"?

　　　　　　　　　　　　　　　　

C 【Key Sentences】 Fill in the blank and translate the following sentences.

重要文について確認しよう【知識・技能】【思考力・判断力・表現力】

② I appreciated now how patient, understanding and kind she was **to have wasted** her time on a little boy.
　◆ appreciate の目的語は疑問詞 how の節。
　◆完了不定詞 to have wasted は，主節の動詞 appreciated よりも以前のことであることを明確にする。
　訳：　　　　　　　　　　　　　　

⑬ I wonder **if** you have any idea **how much** you meant to me during all that time …
　◆接続詞 if は「（1.　　　　　　[日本語で]）」の意味で，wonder の目的語となる節を作る。
　◆疑問詞 how much … は，idea の同格節を導いている。
　訳：　　　　　　　　　　　　　　

111

Part 5 教科書 p.182~p.183 📢意味のまとまりに注意して，本文全体を聞こう。 ◎2-50

① It didn't seem silly, / but I didn't say so. // ② Instead / I told her / how often I had thought of her / over the years, / and I asked / if I could call her again / when I came back / to visit my sister / after the first semester was over. //

③ "Please do. / ④ Just ask for Sally." //

⑤ "Goodbye, / Sally." // ⑥ It sounded strange / for Information Please to have a name. // ⑦ "If I run into any chipmunks, / I'll tell them / to eat fruit and nuts." //

⑧ "Do that," / she said. // ⑨ "And / I expect / one of these days / you'll visit the Orinoco. // ⑩ Well, / goodbye." //

⑪ Just three months later / I was back again / at the Seattle airport. // ⑫ A different voice answered, / "Information," / and I asked for Sally. //

⑬ "Are you a friend?" //

⑭ "Yes," / I said. / ⑮ "An old friend." //

⑯ "Then / I'm sorry / to have to tell you. // ⑰ Sally had only been working part-time / in the last few years / because she was ill. // ⑱ She died five weeks ago." // ⑲ But before I could hang up, / she said, / "Wait a minute. // ⑳ Did you say / your name was Willard?" //

㉑ "Yes." //

㉒ "Well, / Sally left a message / for you. // ㉓ She wrote it down." //

㉔ "What was it?" / I asked, / almost knowing in advance / what it would be. //

㉕ "Here it is, / I'll read it / ── 'Tell him / I still say / there are other worlds / to sing in. // ㉖ He'll know / what I mean.'" //

㉗ I thanked her / and hung up. // ㉘ I did know / what Sally meant. //

📢意味のまとまりに注意して，本文全体を音読しよう。 (235 Words)

Words and Phrases	新出単語・表現の意味を調べよう		
semester 名 [səméstər] A2	1.	**Sally** [sǽli]	サリー
be sorry to 〜	2.	**Willard** [wílərd]	ウィラード
leave A for B	3.		

A 【Comprehension 1】 Fill in the blanks in Japanese.

要点を整理しよう【思考力・判断力・表現力】

ポールが大学生のとき
一学期が終わった後, (1.　　　　　　　) に会うためにシアトルに帰る際に電話することを約束した。 インフォメーション・プリーズの本名が (2.　　　　　　　) とわかった。
3か月後
電話をかけると, (2.　　　　　　　) とは別の人が出た。 ➡(2.　　　　　　　) は (3.　　　　　　　) 前に亡くなったと告げられた。 ➡メッセージが残されていた。ポールが幼いころ, ペットの (4.　　　　　　　) が死んだとき 　に送られたものだった。

B 【Comprehension 2】 Answer the following questions in English.

本文のポイントについて答えよう【思考力・判断力・表現力】

1. When was Paul going to call Sally again?

2. How long did Sally survive after Paul made his last call?

3. Where was Paul likely to go after hanging up the phone?

C 【Key Sentences】 Translate the following sentences.

重要文について確認しよう【知識・技能】【思考力・判断力・表現力】

⑰ Sally **had** only **been working** part-time in the last few years because she was ill.

◆過去完了進行形には, 過去のある時点の直前まで継続中だった動作を表す用法がある。

訳：

㉘ I **did** know what Sally meant.

◆ did は強調を表す助動詞で, 音読のときは強く発音する。

訳：